Encyclical Letter
of Pope Pius XII

THE
SACRED LITURGY

Mediator Dei

St. Paul Books & Media

Vatican Library Translation

ISBN 0-8198-6924-4

Printed and published in the U.S.A. by St. Paul Books & Media
50 St. Paul's Avenue, Boston, MA 02130

St. Paul Books & Media is the publishing house of the Daughters of St. Paul, an international congregation of women religious serving the Church with the communications media.

To Our Venerable Brethren

The Patriarchs, Primates, Archbishops, Bishops and other Ordinaries in Peace and Communion with the Apostolic See

POPE PIUS XII

Venerable Brethren
Health and Apostolic Benediction

INTRODUCTION

Jesus Christ Redeemer of the World

1. Mediator between God and men[1] and High Priest Who has gone before us into heaven, Jesus the Son of God[2] quite clearly had one aim in view when He undertook the mission of mercy which was to endow mankind with the rich blessings of supernatural grace. Sin had disturbed the right relationship between man and his Creator; the Son of God would restore it. The children of Adam were wretched heirs to the infection of original sin; He would bring them back to their Heavenly Father, the primal Source and final Destiny of all things. For this reason He was not content, while He dwelt with us on earth, merely to give notice that Redemption had begun, and to proclaim the long-awaited Kingdom of God, but gave Himself besides in prayer and sacrifice to the task of saving souls, even to the point of offering Himself, as He hung from the Cross, a Victim unspotted unto God, to purify our conscience of dead works, to serve the living God.[3] Thus happily were all men summoned back from the byways leading them down to ruin and disaster, to be set squarely once again upon the path that leads to God. Thanks to the shedding of the Blood of the Immaculate Lamb, now each might set about the personal task of achieving his own sanctification, so rendering to God the glory due to Him.

The Church continues the priestly office of Jesus Christ

2. But what is more, the Divine Redeemer has so willed it that the priestly life begun with the supplication

and sacrifice of His mortal Body should continue without intermission down the ages in His Mystical Body which is the Church. That is why He establishe a visible priesthood to offer everywhere the clean oblation [4] which would enable men from East to West, freed from the shackles of sin, to offer God that unconstrained and voluntary homage which their conscience dictates.

3. In obedience, therefore, to her Founder's behest, the Church prolongs the priestly mission of Jesus Christ mainly by means of the sacred Liturgy. She does this in the first place at the altar, where constantly the Sacrifice of the Cross is re-presented [5] and, with a single difference in the manner of its offering, renewed. [6] She does it next by means of the Sacraments, those special channels through which men are made partakers in the supernatural life. She does it finally by offering to God, all Good and Great, the daily tribute of her prayer of praise. "What a spectacle for heaven and earth," observes Our Predecessor of happy memory, Pius XI, "is not the Church at prayer! For centuries without interruption, from midnight to midnight, the divine psalmody of the inspired canticles is repeated on earth; there is no hour of the day that is not hallowed by its special liturgy; there is no stage of human life that has not its part in the thanksgiving, praise, supplication and reparation of this common prayer of the Mystical Body of Christ which is His Church!" [7]

Revival of liturgical studies

4. You are of course familiar with the fact, Venerable Brethren, that a remarkably widespread revival of scholarly interest in the sacred Liturgy took place towards the end of the last century and has continued through the early years of this one. The movement owed its rise to commendable private initiative and more particularly to the zealous and persistent labor of several monasteries within the distinguished Order of Saint Benedict. Thus there developed in this field among many European nations and in lands beyond the seas as well, a rivalry as welcome as it

was productive of results. Indeed, the salutary fruits of this rivalry among the scholars were plain for all to see, both in the sphere of the Sacred Sciences, where the liturgical rites of the Western and Eastern Church were made the object of extensive research and profound study, and in the spiritual life of considerable numbers of individual Christians.

5. The majestic ceremonies of the Sacrifice of the altar became better known, understood and appreciated. With more widespread and more frequent reception of the Sacraments, the worship of the Eucharist came to be regarded for what it really is: the fountainhead of genuine Christian devotion. Bolder relief was given likewise to the fact that all the faithful make up a single and very compact body with Christ for its Head, and that the Christian community is in duty bound to participate in the liturgical rites according to their station.

Provision of the Holy See for Liturgical Worship

6. You are surely well aware that this Apostolic See has always made careful provision for the schooling of the people committed to its charge in the correct spirit and practice of the Liturgy; and that it has been no less careful to insist that the sacred rites should be performed with due external dignity. In this connection We Ourselves in the course of Our traditional address to the Lenten Preachers of this gracious City of Rome in 1943, urged them warmly to exhort their respective hearers to more faithful participation in the Eucharistic Sacrifice. Only a short while previously, with the design of rendering the prayers of the Liturgy more correctly understood and their truth and unction more easy to perceive, We arranged to have the Book of Psalms, which forms such an important part of these prayers in the Catholic Church, translated once more into Latin from their original text. [8]

7. But while We derive no little satisfaction from the wholesome results of the movement just described, duty obliges Us to give serious attention to this "revival" as it is

advocated in some quarters, and to take proper steps to preserve it at the outset from excess or outright perversion.

Deficiencies of some ... Exaggerations of others

8. Indeed, though We are sorely grieved to note, on the one hand, that there are places where the spirit, understanding or practice of the sacred Liturgy is defective, or all but inexistent, We observe with considerable anxiety and some misgiving, that elsewhere certain enthusiasts, over eager in their search for novelty, are straying beyond the path of sound doctrine and prudence. Not seldom, in fact, they interlard their plans and hopes for a revival of the sacred Liturgy with principles which compromise this holiest of causes in theory or practice, and sometimes even taint it with errors touching Catholic faith and ascetical doctrine.

9. Yet the integrity of faith and morals ought to be the special criterion of this sacred science, which must conform exactly to what the Church out of the abundance of her wisdom teaches and prescribes. It is consequently Our prerogative to commend and approve whatever is done properly, and to check or censure any aberration from the path of truth and rectitude.

10. Let not the apathetic or half-hearted imagine, however, that We agree with them when We reprove the erring and restrain the overbold. No more must the imprudent think that We are commending them when We correct the faults of those who are negligent and sluggish.

11. If in this Encyclical Letter We treat chiefly of the Latin Liturgy, it is not because We esteem less highly the venerable Liturgies of the Eastern Church, whose ancient and honorable ritual traditions are just as dear to Us. The reason lies rather in a special situation prevailing in the Western Church, of sufficient importance, it would seem, to require this exercise of Our Authority.

12. With docile hearts, then, let all Christians hearken to the voice of their Common Father, who would have them, each and every one, intimately united with him as

they approach the altar of God, professing the same faith, obedient to the same law, sharing in the same Sacrifice with a single intention and one sole desire. This is a duty imposed, of course, by the honor due to God. But the needs of our day and age demand it as well. After a long and cruel war which has rent whole peoples asunder with its rivalry and slaughter, men of good will are spending themselves in the effort to find the best possible way to restore peace to the world. It is, notwithstanding, Our belief that no plan or initiative can offer better prospect of success than that fervent religious spirit and zeal by which Christians must be formed and guided; in this way their common and whole-hearted acceptance of the same truth, along with their united obedience and loyalty to their appointed pastors while rendering to God the worship due to Him, makes of them one brotherhood: "for we, being many, are one body: all that partake of one bread." [9]

PART I

THE NATURE, SOURCE AND DEVELOPMENT OF THE LITURGY

I. THE LITURGY IS PUBLIC WORSHIP

To honor God: The duty of individuals

13. It is unquestionably the fundamental duty of man to orientate his person and his life towards God. "For He it is to Whom we must first be bound, as to an unfailing principle; to Whom even our free choice must be directed as to an ultimate objective. It is He, too, Whom we lose when carelessly we sin. It is He Whom we must recover by our faith and trust." [10] But man turns properly to God when he acknowledges His supreme majesty and supreme authority; when he accepts divinely revealed truths with a submissive mind; when he scrupulously obeys divine law, centering in God his every act and aspiration; when he accords, in short, due worship to the One True God by practicing the virtue of religion.

The duty of the community

14. This duty is incumbent, first of all, on men as individuals. But it also binds the whole community of human beings, grouped together by mutual social ties: mankind, too, depends on the sovereign authority of God.

15. It should be noted, moreover, that men are bound by this obligation in a special way in virtue of the fact that God has raised them to the supernatural order.

16. Thus we observe that when God institutes the Old Law, He makes provision besides for sacred rites, and determines in exact detail the rules to be observed by His people in rendering Him the worship He ordains. To this end He established various kinds of sacrifice and designated the ceremonies with which they were to be offered to Him. His enactments on all matters relating to the Ark of the Covenant, the Temple and the Holy Days are minute and clear. He established a sacerdotal tribe with its high priest, selected and described the vestments with which the sacred ministers were to be clothed and every function in any way pertaining to divine worship.[11] Yet, this was nothing more than a faint foreshadowing[12] of the worship which the High Priest of the New Testament was to render to the Father in heaven.

Honor given to the Father
by the Incarnate Word ... on Earth

17. No sooner, in fact, "is the Word made flesh"[13] than He shows Himself to the world vested with a priestly office, making to the Eternal Father an act of submission which will continue uninterruptedly as long as He lives: "When He cometh into the world He saith . . . 'behold I come . . . to do Thy will'."[14] This act He was to consummate admirably in the bloody Sacrifice of the Cross: "In the which 'will' we are sanctified by the oblation of the Body of Jesus Christ once."[15] He plans His active life among men with no other purpose in view. As a Child He is presented to the Lord in the Temple. To the Temple He returns as a grown Boy, and often afterwards to instruct

the people and to pray. He fasts for forty days before beginning His public ministry. His counsel and example summon all to prayer, daily and at night as well. As Teacher of the truth He "enlighteneth every man" [16] to the end that mortals may duly acknowledge the immortal God, "not withdrawing unto perdition, but faithful to the saving of the soul." [17] As Shepherd He watches over His flock, leads it to life-giving pasture, and lays down a law that none shall wander from His side, off the straight path He has pointed out, and that all shall lead holy lives imbued with His spirit and moved by His active aid. At the Last Supper He celebrates a New Pasch with solemn rite and ceremonial, and provides for its continuance through the divine institution of the Eucharist. On the morrow, lifted up between heaven and earth, He offers the saving Sacrifice of His life, and pours forth, as it were, from His pierced Heart the Sacraments destined to impart the treasures of Redemption to the souls of men. All this He does with but a single aim: the glory of His Father and man's ever greater sanctification.

... in Heaven

18. But it is His will, besides, that the worship He instituted and practiced during His life on earth shall continue ever afterwards without any intermission. For He has not left mankind an orphan. He still offers us the support of His powerful, unfailing intercession, acting as our "advocate with the Father." [18] He aids us likewise through His Church, where He is present indefectibly as the ages run their course; through the Church which He constituted "the pillar of truth," [19] and dispenser of grace, and which, by His sacrifice on the Cross, He founded, consecrated and confirmed forever. [20]

In union with Christ, the Church continues to honor God

19. The Church has, therefore, in common with the Word Incarnate the aim, the obligation and the function of teaching all men the truth, of governing and directing

them aright, of offering to God the pleasing and acceptable Sacrifice; in this way the Church reestablishes between the Creator and His creatures that unity and harmony to which the Apostle of the Gentiles alludes in these words: "Now, therefore, you are no more strangers and foreigners; but you are fellow citizens with the saints and domestics of God, built upon the foundations of the apostles and the prophets, Jesus Christ Himself being the chief corner stone: in Whom all the building, being framed together, groweth up into a holy temple in the Lord, in Whom you also are built together into a habitation of God in the Spirit." [21] Thus the society founded by the Divine Redeemer, whether in her doctrine and government, or in the Sacrifice and Sacraments instituted by Him, or finally, in the ministry, which He has confided to her charge with the outpouring of His prayer and the shedding of His blood, has no other goal or purpose than to increase ever in strength and unity.

20. This result is in fact achieved when Christ lives and thrives, as it were, in the hearts of men, and when men's hearts in turn are fashioned and expanded as though by Christ. This makes it possible for the sacred temple, where the Divine Majesty receives the acceptable worship which His law prescribes, to increase and prosper day by day in this land of exile on earth. Along with the Church, therefore, her divine Founder is present at every liturgical function: Christ is present at the august Sacrifice of the altar both in the person of His minister and above all under the Eucharistic species. He is present in the Sacraments, infusing into them the power which makes them ready instruments of sanctification. He is present finally in the prayer of praise and petition we direct to God, as it is written: "Where there are two or three gathered together in My Name, there am I in the midst of them." [22] The sacred Liturgy is consequently the public worship which our Redeemer as Head of the Church renders to the Father as well as the worship which the community of the faithful renders to its Founder, and through Him to the Heavenly

Father. It is, in short, the worship rendered by the Mystical Body of Christ in the entirety of its Head and members.

Historical beginnings of the sacred Liturgy

21. Liturgical practice begins with the very founding of the Church. The first Christians, in fact, "were persevering in the doctrine of the apostles and in the communication of the breaking of bread and in prayers." [23] Whenever their Pastors can summon a little group of the faithful together, they set up an altar on which they proceed to offer the Sacrifice, and around which are ranged all the other rites appropriate for the saving of souls and for the honor due to God. Among these latter rites, the first place is reserved for the Sacraments, namely the seven principal founts of salvation. There follows the celebration of the divine praises in which the faithful also join, obeying the behest of the Apostle Paul: "In all wisdom: teaching and admonishing one another in psalms, hymns and spiritual canticles, singing in grace in your hearts to God." [24] Next comes the reading of the Law, the Prophets, the Gospel and the Apostolic Epistles; and last of all the homily or sermon in which the official head of the congregation recalls and explains the practical bearing of the commandments of the Divine Master and the chief events of His life, combining instruction with appropriate exhortation and illustration for the benefit of all his listeners.

Its organization and developments

22. As circumstances and the needs of the Christians warrant, public worship is organized, developed and enriched by new rites, ceremonies and regulations, always with the singular end in view: "that we may use these external signs to keep us alert, learn from them what distance we have come along the road, and by them be heartened to go on further with more eager step; for the effect will be more precious the warmer the affection which precedes it." [25] Here then is a better and more suitable way to raise the heart to God. Thenceforth the priesthood of Jesus Christ is a living and continuous reality

through all the ages to the end of time, since the Liturgy is nothing more nor less than the exercise of this priestly function. Like her divine Head, the Church is forever present in the midst of her children. She aids and exhorts them to holiness, so that they may one day return to the Father in heaven clothed with that beauteous raiment of the supernatural. To all who are born to life on earth she gives a second, supernatural kind of birth. She arms them with the Holy Spirit for the struggle against the implacable enemy. She gathers all Christians about her altars, inviting and urging them repeatedly to take part in the celebration of the Mass, feeding them with the Bread of Angels to make them ever stronger. She purifies and consoles the hearts that sin has wounded and soiled. Solemnly she consecrates those whom God has called to the priestly ministry. She fortifies with new gifts of grace the chaste nuptials of those who are destined to found and bring up a Christian family. When at last she has soothed and refreshed the closing hours of this earthly life by Holy Viaticum and Extreme Unction, with the utmost affection she accompanies the mortal remains of her children to the grave, lays them reverently to rest, and confides them to the protection of the Cross, against the day when they will triumph over death and rise again. She has a further solemn blessing and invocation for those of her children who dedicate themselves to the service of God in the life of religious perfection. Finally, she extends to the souls in Purgatory who implore her intercession and her prayers the helping hand which may lead them happily at last to eternal blessedness in heaven.

II. THE LITURGY IS EXTERIOR AND INTERIOR WORSHIP

Exterior Worship

23. The worship rendered by the Church to God must be, in its entirety, interior as well as exterior. It is exterior because the nature of man as a composite body and soul requires it to be so. Likewise, because Divine Providence has disposed that "while we recognize God visibly, we

may be drawn by Him to love of things unseen." [26] Every impulse of the human heart, besides, expresses itself naturally through the senses; and the worship of God, being the concern not merely of individuals but of the whole community of mankind, must therefore be social as well. This obviously it cannot be unless religious activity is also organized and manifested outwardly. Exterior worship finally, reveals and emphasizes the unity of the Mystical Body, feeds new fuel to its holy zeal, fortifies its energy, intensifies its action day by day: "for although the ceremonies themselves can claim no perfection or sanctity in their own right, they are, nevertheless, the outward acts of religion, designed to rouse the heart, like signals of a sort, to veneration of the sacred realities, and to raise the mind to meditation on the supernatural. They serve to foster piety, to kindle the flame of charity, to increase our faith and deepen our devotion. They provide instruction for simple folk, decoration for divine worship, continuity of religious practice. They make it possible to tell genuine Christians from their false or heretical counterparts." [27]

But it is especially interior worship

24. But the chief element of divine worship must be interior. For we must always live in Christ and give ourselves to Him completely, so that in Him, with Him and through Him the heavenly Father may be duly glorified. The sacred Liturgy requires, however, that both of these elements be intimately linked with each other. This recommendation the Liturgy itself is careful to repeat, as often as it prescribes an exterior act of worship. Thus we are urged, when there is question of fasting, for example "to give interior effect to our outward observance." [28] Otherwise religion clearly amounts to mere formalism, without meaning and without content. You recall, Venerable Brethren, how the Divine Master expels from the sacred Temple, as unworthy to worship there, people who pretend to honor God with nothing but neat and well-turned phrases, like actors in a theater, and think themselves perfectly

capable of working out their eternal salvation without plucking their inveterate vices from their hearts.[29] It is, therefore, the keen desire of the Church that all of the faithful kneel at the feet of the Redeemer to tell Him how much they venerate and love Him. She wants them present in crowds—like the children whose joyous cries accompanied His entry into Jerusalem—to sing their hymns and chant their song of praise and thanksgiving to Him Who is King of Kings and Source of every blessing. She would have them move their lips in prayer, sometimes in petition, sometimes in joy and gratitude, and in this way experience His merciful aid and power like the Apostles at the lakeside of Tiberias, or abandon themselves totally, like Peter on Mount Thabor, to mystic union with the Eternal God in contemplation.

Exaggeration of the external element

25. It is an error consequently and a mistake to think of the sacred Liturgy as merely the outward or visible part of divine worship or as an ornamental ceremonial. No less erroneous is the notion that it consists solely in a list of laws and prescriptions according to which the ecclesiastical Hierarchy orders the sacred rites to be performed.

26. It should be clear to all, then, that God cannot be honored worthily unless the mind and heart turn to Him in quest of the perfect life, and that the worship rendered to God by the Church in union with her divine Head is the most efficacious means of achieving sanctity.

27. This efficacy, where there is question of the Eucharistic Sacrifice and the Sacraments, derives first of all and principally from the act itself *(ex opere operato)*. But if one considers the part which the Immaculate Spouse of Jesus Christ takes in the action, embellishing the Sacrifice and Sacraments with prayer and sacred ceremonies, or if one refers to the "Sacramentals" and the other rites instituted by the Hierarchy of the Church, then its effectiveness is due rather to the action of the Church *(ex opere operantis Ecclesiae),* inasmuch as she is holy and acts always in closest union with her Head.

New theories on "objective piety"

28. In this connection, Venerable Brethren, We desire to direct your attention to certain recent theories touching a so-called "objective" piety. While these theories attempt, it is true, to throw light on the mystery of the Mystical Body, on the effective reality of sanctifying grace, on the action of God in the Sacraments and in the Mass, it is nonetheless apparent that they tend to belittle, or pass over in silence, what they call "subjective," or "personal" piety.

29. It is an unquestionable fact that the work of our Redemption is continued, and that its fruits are imparted to us, during the celebration of the Liturgy, notably in the august Sacrifice of the altar. Christ acts each day to save us, in the Sacraments and in His holy Sacrifice. By means of them He is constantly atoning for the sins of mankind, constantly consecrating it to God. Sacraments and Sacrifice do, then, possess that "objective" power to make us really and personally sharers in the divine life of Jesus Christ. Not from any ability of our own, but by the power of God, are they endowed with the capacity to unite the piety of members with that of the Head, and to make this, in a sense, the action of the whole community. From these profound considerations some are led to conclude that all Christian piety must be centered in the mystery of the Mystical Body of Christ, with no regard for what is "personal" or "subjective," as they would have it. As a result they feel that all other religious exercises not directly connected with the sacred Liturgy and performed outside public worship, should be omitted.

30. But though the principles set forth above are excellent, it must be plain to everyone that the conclusions drawn from them respecting the two sorts of piety are false, insidious, and quite pernicious.

Necessity of personal piety

31. Very truly, the Sacraments and the Sacrifice of the altar, being Christ's own actions, must be held to be capa-

ble in themselves of conveying and dispensing grace from the divine Head to the members of the Mystical Body. But if they are to produce their proper effect, it is absolutely necessary that our hearts be rightly disposed to receive them. Hence the warning of Paul the Apostle with reference to Holy Communion: "But let a man first prove himself; and then let him eat of this bread and drink of the chalice." [30] This explains why the Church in a brief and significant phrase calls the various acts of mortification, especially those practiced during the season of Lent, "the Christian army's defenses." [31] They represent, in fact, the personal effort and activity of members who desire, as grace urges and aids them, to join forces with their Captain—"that we may discover... in our Captain," to borrow Saint Augustine's words, "the fountain of grace itself." [32] But observe that these members are alive, endowed and equipped with an intelligence and will of their own. It follows that they are strictly required to put their own lips to the fountain, imbibe and absorb for themselves the life-giving water, and rid themselves personally of anything that might hinder its nutritive effect in their souls. Emphatically, therefore, the work of Redemption, which in itself is independent of our will, requires a serious interior effort on our part if we are to achieve eternal salvation.

Necessity of meditation and spiritual exercises

32. If the private and interior devotion of individuals were to neglect the august Sacrifice of the altar and the Sacraments, and to withdraw them from the stream of vital energy that flows from Head to members, it would indeed be sterile, and deserves to be condemned. But when devotional exercises, and pious practices in general, not strictly connected with the sacred Liturgy, confine themselves to merely human acts, with the express purpose of directing these latter to the Father in Heaven, of rousing people to repentance and holy fear of God, of weaning them from seductions of the world and its vice, and

leading them back to the difficult path of perfection, then certainly such practices are not only highly praiseworthy but absolutely indispensable; because they expose the dangers threatening the spiritual life; they promote the acquisition of virtue; and because they increase the fervor and generosity with which we are bound to dedicate all that we are and all that we have to the service of Jesus Christ. Genuine and real piety, which the Angelic Doctor calls "devotion," and which is the principal act of the virtue of religion—that act which correctly relates and fitly directs men to God and by which they freely and spontaneously give themselves to the worship of God in its fullest sense [33]—piety of this authentic sort needs meditation on the supernatural realities and spiritual exercises, if it is to be nurtured, stimulated and sustained, and if it is to prompt us to lead a more perfect life. For the Christian religion, practiced as it should be, demands that the will especially be consecrated to God and exert its influence on all the other spiritual faculties. But every act of the will presupposes an act of the intelligence, and before one can express the desire and the intention of offering oneself in sacrifice to the eternal Godhead, a knowledge of the facts and truths which make religion a duty is altogether necessary. One must first know, for instance, man's last end and the supremacy of the Divine Majesty; after that, our common duty of submission to our Creator; and finally the inexhaustible treasures of love with which God yearns to enrich us, as well as the necessity of supernatural grace for the achievement of our destiny, and that special path marked out for us by Divine Providence in virtue of the fact that we have been united one and all, like members of a body, to Jesus Christ the Head. But further, since our hearts, disturbed as they are at times by the lower appetites, do not always respond to motives of love, it is also extremely helpful to let consideration and contemplation of the justice of God provoke us on occasion to salutary fear, and guide us thence to Christian humility, repentance and amendment.

The concrete results of piety

33. But it will not do to possess these facts and truths after the fashion of an abstract memory lesson or lifeless commentary. They must lead to practical results. They must impel us to subject our senses and their faculties to reason, as illuminated by the Catholic faith. They must help to cleanse and purify the heart uniting it to Christ more intimately every day, growing ever more in His likeness, and drawing from Him the divine inspiration and strength of which it stands in need. They must serve as increasingly effective incentives to action; urging men to produce good fruit, to perform their individual duties faithfully, to give themselves eagerly to the regular practice of their religion and the energetic exercise of virtue. "You are Christ's, and Christ is God's." [34] Let everything, therefore, have its proper place and arrangement; let everything be "theocentric" so to speak, if we really wish to direct everything to the glory of God through the life and power which flows from the divine Head into our hearts: "Having therefore, brethren, a confidence in the entering into the holies by the Blood of Christ, a new and living way which He both dedicated for us through the veil, that is to say, His flesh, and a high priest over the house of God; let us draw near with a true heart, in fulness of faith, having our hearts sprinkled from an evil conscience and our bodies washed with clean water, let us hold fast the confession of our hope without wavering... and let us consider one another, to provoke unto charity and to good works." [35]

Harmony and equilibrium among the members of the Mystical Body

34. Here is the source of the harmony and equilibrium which prevails among the members of the Mystical Body of Jesus Christ. When the Church teaches us our Catholic faith and exhorts us to obey the commandments of Christ, she is paving a way for her priestly, sanctifying action in its highest sense; she disposes us likewise for more serious meditation on the life of the Divine Redeemer and guides

us to profounder knowledge of the mysteries of faith where we may draw the supernatural sustenance, strength and vitality that enable us to progress safely, through Christ, towards a more perfect life. Not only through her ministers, but with the help of the faithful individually, who have imbibed in this fashion the spirit of Christ, the Church endeavors to permeate with this same spirit the life and labors of men—their private and family life, their social, even economic and political life—that all who are called God's children may reach more readily the end He has proposed for them.

35. Such action on the part of individual Christians, then, along with the ascetic effort prompting them to purify their hearts, actually stimulates in the faithful those energies which enable them to participate in the august Sacrifice of the altar with better dispositions. They now can receive the Sacraments with more abundant fruit, and come from the celebration of the sacred rites more eager, more firmly resolved to pray and deny themselves like Christians, to answer the inspirations and invitation of divine grace and to imitate daily more closely, the virtues of our Redeemer. And all of this not simply for their own advantage, but for that of the whole Church, where whatever good is accomplished proceeds from the power of her Head and redounds to the advancement of all her members.

Agreement between divine action and human cooperation

36. In the spiritual life, consequently, there can be no opposition between the action of God, Who pours forth His grace into men's hearts so that the work of the Redemption may always abide, and the tireless collaboration of man, who must not render vain the gift of God. [36] No more can the efficacy of the external administration of the Sacraments, which comes from the rite itself *(ex opere operato)*, be opposed to the meritorious action of their ministers or recipients, which we call the agent's action

(opus operantis). Similarly, no conflict exists between public prayer and prayers in private, between morality and contemplation, between the ascetical life and devotion to the Liturgy. Finally there is no opposition between the jurisdiction and teaching office of the ecclesiastical Hierarchy, and the specifically priestly power exercised in the sacred ministry.

37. Considering their special designation to perform the liturgical functions of the Holy Sacrifice and Divine Office, the Church has serious reasons for prescribing that the ministers she assigns to the service of the sanctuary and members of religious institutes betake themselves at stated times to mental prayer, to examination of conscience, and to various other spiritual exercises. [37] Unquestionably liturgical prayer, being the public supplication of the illustrious Spouse of Jesus Christ, is superior in excellence to private prayers. But this superior worth does not at all imply contrast or incompatibility between these two kinds of prayer. For both merge harmoniously in the single spirit which animates them: "Christ is all and in all." [38] Both tend to the same objective: until Christ be formed in us. [39]

III. THE LITURGY UNDER THE HIERARCHY OF THE CHURCH

The nature of the Church requires a Hierarchy

38. For a better and more accurate understanding of the sacred Liturgy another of its characteristic features, no less important, needs to be considered.

39. The Church is a society, and as such requires an authority and Hierarchy of her own. Though it is true that all the members of the Mystical Body partake of the same blessings and pursue the same objective, they do not all enjoy the same powers, nor are they all qualified to perform the same acts. The Divine Redeemer has willed as a matter of fact, that His Kingdom should be built and solidly supported, as it were, on a holy order, which resembles in some sort the heavenly Hierarchy.

40. Only to the Apostles, and thenceforth to those on whom their successors have imposed hands, is granted the power of the priesthood, in virtue of which they represent the person of Jesus Christ before their people, acting at the same time as representatives of their people before God. This priesthood is not transmitted by heredity or human descent. It does not emanate from the Christian community. It is not a delegation from the people. Prior to acting as representative of the community before the throne of God, the priest is the ambassador of the Divine Redeemer. He is God's vicegerent in the midst of his flock precisely because Jesus Christ is Head of that Body of which Christians are the members. The power entrusted to him, therefore, bears no natural resemblance to anything human. It is entirely supernatural. It comes from God. "As the Father hath sent me, I also send you"... [40] "he that heareth you heareth me"... [41] "go ye into the whole world and preach the gospel to every creature; he that believeth and is baptized shall be saved." [42]

... and hence a visible external priesthood

41. That is why the visible, external priesthood of Jesus Christ is not handed down indiscriminately to all members of the Church in general, but is conferred on designated men, through what may be called the spiritual generation of Holy Orders.

42. This latter, one of the seven Sacraments, not only imparts the grace appropriate to the clerical function and state of life, but imparts an indelible "character" besides, indicating the sacred ministers' conformity to Jesus Christ the Priest, and qualifying them to perform these official acts of religion by which men are sanctified and God is duly glorified in keeping with the divine laws and regulations.

Consecrated by the Sacrament of Holy Orders

43. In the same way, actually, that Baptism is the distinctive mark of all Christians, and serves to differentiate them from those who have not been cleansed in this

purifying stream and consequently are not members of Christ, the Sacrament of Holy Orders sets the priest apart from the rest of the faithful who have not received this consecration. For they alone, in answer to an inward supernatural call have entered the august ministry, where they are assigned to service in the sanctuary and become, as it were, the instruments God uses to communicate supernatural life from on high to the Mystical Body of Jesus Christ. Add to this, as We have noted above, the fact that they alone have been marked with the indelible sign "conforming" them to Christ the Priest, and that their hands alone have been consecrated "in order that whatever they bless may be blessed, whatever they consecrate may become sacred and holy, in the name of Our Lord Jesus Christ." [43] Let all then who would live in Christ, flock to their priests. By them they will be supplied with the comforts and food of the spiritual life. From them they will procure the medicine of salvation assuring their cure and happy recovery from the fatal sickness of their sins. The priest, finally, will bless their homes, consecrate their families and help them, as they breathe their last, across the threshold of eternal happiness.

The Liturgy depends on Ecclesiastical Authority

a) by its very nature

44. Since therefore it is the priest chiefly who performs the sacred Liturgy in the name of the Church, its organization, regulation and details cannot but be subject to Church authority. This conclusion, based on the nature of Christian worship itself, is further confirmed by the testimony of history.

b) by its close connection with dogma

45. Additional proof of this indefeasible right of the Ecclesiastical Hierarchy lies in the circumstance that the sacred Liturgy is intimately bound up with doctrinal propositions which the Church proposes as perfectly true and certain, and must as a consequence conform to the decrees respecting Catholic faith issued by the Supreme

Teaching Authority of the Church with a view to safeguarding the integrity of the religion revealed by God.

46. On this subject We judge it Our duty to rectify an attitude with which you are doubtless familiar, Venerable Brethren. We refer to the error and fallacious reasoning of those who have claimed that the sacred Liturgy is a kind of proving-ground for the truths to be held of faith, meaning by this that the Church is obliged to declare such a doctrine sound when it is found to have produced fruits of piety and sanctity through the sacred rites of Liturgy, and to reject it otherwise. Hence the epigram: *"Lex orandi, lex credendi"*—the law for prayer is the law for faith.

47. But this is not what the Church teaches and enjoins. The worship she offers to God, all Good and Great, is a continuous profession of Catholic faith and a continuous exercise of hope and charity, as Augustine puts it tersely: "God is to be worshipped," he says, "by faith, hope and charity." [44] In the sacred Liturgy we profess the Catholic faith explicitly and openly, not only by the celebration of the mysteries, and by offering the Holy Sacrifice and administering the Sacraments, but also by saying or singing the Credo or Symbol of the Faith—it is indeed the sign and badge, as it were, of the Christian—along with other texts, and likewise by the reading of Holy Scripture, written under the inspiration of the Holy Ghost. The entire Liturgy, therefore, has the Catholic faith for its content, inasmuch as it bears public witness to the faith of the Church.

48. For this reason, whenever there was question of defining a truth revealed by God, the Sovereign Pontiff and the Councils in their recourse to the "theological sources," as they are called, have not seldom drawn many an argument from this sacred science of the Liturgy. For an example in point, Our Predecessor of immortal memory, Pius IX, so argued when he proclaimed the Immaculate Conception of the Virgin Mary. Similarly during the discussion of a doubtful or controversial truth, the Church and the Holy Fathers have not failed to look to the age-old and age-honored sacred rites for enlightenment.

Hence the well-known and venerable maxim: *"Legem credendi lex statuat supplicandi"* —let the rule for prayer determine the rule of belief. [45] The sacred Liturgy consequently, does not decide or determine independently and of itself what is of Catholic faith. More properly, since the Liturgy is also a profession of eternal truths, and subject, as such, to the Supreme Teaching Authority of the Church, it can supply proofs and testimony, quite clearly of no little value, towards the determination of a particular point of Christian doctrine. But if one desires to differentiate and describe the relationship between faith and the sacred Liturgy in absolute and general terms, it is perfectly correct to say: *"Lex credendi legem statuat supplicandi"*—let the rule of belief determine the rule of prayer. The same holds true for the other theological virtues also: *"In ... fide, spe, caritate continuato desiderio semper oramus*—we pray always, with constant yearning in faith, hope and charity." [46]

IV. PROGRESS AND DEVELOPMENT OF THE LITURGY

49. From time immemorial the Ecclesiastical Hierarchy has exercised this right in matters liturgical. It has organized and regulated divine worship, enriching it constantly with new splendor and beauty, to the glory of God and the spiritual profit of Christians. What is more, it has not been slow—keeping the substance of the Mass and Sacraments carefully intact—to modify what it deemed not altogether fitting, and to add what appeared more likely to increase the honor paid to Jesus Christ and the august Trinity, and to instruct and stimulate the Christian people to greater advantage. [47]

Divine and human elements in the Liturgy

50. The sacred Liturgy does in fact include divine as well as human elements. The former, instituted as they have been by God, cannot be changed in any way by men. But the human components admit of various modifications, as the needs of the age, circumstance and the good of souls may require, and as the Ecclesiastical Hierarchy under

guidance of the Holy Spirit, may have authorized. This will explain the marvellous variety of Eastern and Western rites. Here is the reason for the gradual addition, through successive development, of particular religious customs and practices of piety only faintly discernible in earlier times. Hence likewise it happens from time to time that certain devotions long since forgotten are revived and practiced anew. All these developments attest the abiding life of the Immaculate Spouse of Jesus Christ through these many centuries. They are the sacred language she uses, as the ages run their course, to profess to her divine Spouse her own faith, along with that of the nations committed to her charge, and her own unfailing love. They furnish proof, besides, of the wisdom of the teaching method she employs to arouse and nourish constantly the "Christian instinct."

51. Several causes, really, have been instrumental in the progress and development of the sacred Liturgy during the long and glorious life of the Church.

Development of some human elements
a) due to a more explicit formulation of doctrine

52. Thus for example, as Catholic doctrine on the Incarnate Word of God, the Eucharistic Sacrament and Sacrifice, and Mary the Virgin Mother of God came to be determined with greater certitude and clarity, new ritual forms were introduced through which the acts of the Liturgy proceeded to reproduce this brighter light issuing from the decrees of the teaching Authority of the Church, and to reflect it, in a sense, so that it might reach the minds and hearts of Christ's people more readily.

b) due to disciplinary modifications

53. The subsequent advances in ecclesiastical discipline for the administering of the Sacraments, that of Penance for example; the institution and later suppression of the Catechumenate; and again, the practice of Eucharistic Communion under a single species, adopted in the Latin Church; these developments were assuredly respon-

sible in no little measure for the modification of the ancient ritual in the course of time, and for the gradual introduction of new rites considered more in accord with prevailing discipline in these matters.

c) due also to non-liturgical practices

54. Just as notable a contribution to this progressive transformation was made by devotional trends and practices not directly related to the sacred Liturgy, which began to appear, by God's wonderful design, in later periods, and grew to be so popular. We may instance the spread and ever mounting ardor of devotion to the Blessed Eucharist, devotion to the most bitter Passion of Our Redeemer, devotion to the most Sacred Heart of Jesus, to the Virgin Mother of God and to her most chaste Spouse.

55. Other manifestations of piety have also played their circumstantial part in this same liturgical development. Among them may be cited the public pilgrimages to the tombs of the martyrs prompted by motives of devotion, the special periods of fasting instituted for this same reason, and lastly, in this gracious City of Rome, the penitential recitation of the litanies during the "Station" processions, in which even the Sovereign Pontiff frequently joined.

d) due also to the development of the fine arts

56. It is likewise easy to understand that the progress of the fine arts, those of architecture, painting and music above all, have exerted considerable influence on the choice and disposition of the various external features of the sacred Liturgy.

57. The Church has further used her right of control over liturgical observance to protect the purity of divine worship against abuse from dangerous and imprudent innovations introduced by private individuals and particular churches. Thus it came about—during the 16th century, when usages and customs of this sort had become increasingly prevalent and exaggerated, and when private initiative in matters liturgical threatened to compromise the integrity of faith and devotion, to the great advantage

of heretics and further spread of their errors—that in the year 1588, Our Predecessor Sixtus V of immortal memory established the Sacred Congregation of Rites, charged with the defence of the legitimate rites of the Church and with the prohibition of any spurious innovation.[48] This body fulfills even today the official function of supervision and legislation with regard to all matters touching the sacred Liturgy.[49]

V. ITS DEVELOPMENT
MAY NOT BE LEFT TO PRIVATE JUDGMENT

58. It follows from this that the Sovereign Pontiff alone enjoys the right to recognize and establish any practice touching the worship of God, to introduce and approve new rites, as also to modify those he judges to require modification.[50] Bishops, for their part, have the right and duty carefully to watch over the exact observance of the prescriptions of the sacred canons respecting divine worship.[51] Private individuals, therefore, even though they be clerics, may not be left to decide for themselves in these holy and venerable matters, involving as they do the religious life of Christian society along with the exercise of the priesthood of Jesus Christ and worship of God; concerned as they are with the honor due to the Blessed Trinity, the Word Incarnate and His august Mother and the other Saints, and with the salvation of souls as well. For the same reason no private person has any authority to regulate external practices of this kind, which are intimately bound up with Church discipline and with the order, unity and concord of the Mystical Body and frequently even with the integrity of Catholic faith itself.

Some rash abuses

59. The Church is without question a living organism, and as an organism in respect of the sacred Liturgy also, she grows, matures, develops, adapts and accommodates herself to temporal needs and circumstances, provided only that the integrity of her doctrine be safeguarded. This notwithstanding, the temerity and daring of those who in-

troduce novel liturgical practices, or call for the revival of obsolete rites out of harmony with prevailing laws and rubrics, deserve severe reproof. It has pained Us grievously to note, Venerable Brethren, that such innovations are actually being introduced, not merely in minor details but in matters of major importance as well. We instance, in point of fact, those who make use of the vernacular in the celebration of the august Eucharistic Sacrifice; those who transfer certain feast-days—which have been appointed and established after mature deliberation—to other dates; those finally who delete from the prayer-books approved for public use the sacred texts of the Old Testament, deeming them little suited and inopportune for modern times.

60. The use of the Latin language, customary in a considerable portion of the Church, is a manifest and beautiful sign of unity, as well as an effective antidote for any corruption of doctrinal truth. In spite of this, the use of the mother tongue in connection with several of the rites may be of much advantage to the people. But the Apostolic See alone is empowered to grant this permission. It is forbidden, therefore, to take any action whatever of this nature without having requested and obtained such consent, since the sacred Liturgy, as We have said, is entirely subject to the discretion and approval of the Holy See.

Exaggerated attachment to ancient rites

61. The same reasoning holds in the case of some persons who are bent on the restoration of all the ancient rites and ceremonies indiscriminately. The Liturgy of the early ages is most certainly worthy of all veneration. But ancient usage must not be esteemed more suitable and proper, either in its own right or in its significance for later times and new situations, on the simple ground that it carries the savor and aroma of antiquity. The more recent liturgical rites likewise deserve reverence and respect. They too owe their inspiration to the Holy Spirit, Who assists the Church in every age even to the consummation of the world. [52] They are equally the resources used by

the majestic Spouse of Jesus Christ to promote and procure the sanctity of men.

62. Assuredly it is a wise and most laudable thing to return in spirit and affection to the sources of the sacred Liturgy. For research in this field of study, by tracing it back to its origins, contributes valuable assistance towards a more thorough and careful investigation of the significance of feast-days, and of the meaning of the texts and sacred ceremonies employed on their occasion. But it is neither wise nor laudable to reduce everything to antiquity by every possible device. Thus, to cite some instances, one would be straying from the straight path were he to wish the altar restored to its primitive table-form; were he to want black excluded as a color for the liturgical vestments; were he to forbid the use of sacred images and statues in Churches; were he to order the crucifix so designed that the Divine Redeemer's Body shows no trace of His cruel sufferings; lastly were he to disdain and reject polyphonic music or singing in parts, even where it conforms to regulations issued by the Holy See.

Excessive archaism

63. Clearly no sincere Catholic can refuse to accept the formulation of Christian doctrine more recently elaborated and proclaimed as dogmas by the Church, under the inspiration and guidance of the Holy Spirit with abundant fruit for souls, because it pleases him to hark back to the old formulas. No more can any Catholic in his right senses repudiate existing legislation of the Church to revert to prescriptions based on the earliest sources of canon law. Just as obviously unwise and mistaken is the zeal of one who in matters liturgical, would go back to the rites and usage of antiquity, discarding the new patterns introduced by disposition of Divine Providence to meet the changes of circumstances and situation.

64. This way of acting bids fair to revive the exaggerated and senseless antiquarianism to which the illegal Council of Pistoja gave rise. It likewise attempts to rein-

state a series of errors which were responsible for the calling of that meeting as well as for those resulting from it, with grievous harm to souls, and which the Church, the ever watchful guardian of the "deposit of faith" committed to her charge by her Divine Founder, had every right and reason to condemn. [53] For perverse designs and ventures of this sort tend to paralyze and weaken that process of sanctification by which the sacred Liturgy directs the sons of adoption to their Heavenly Father for their souls' salvation.

65. In every measure taken, then, let proper contact with the Ecclesiastical Hierarchy be maintained. Let no one arrogate to himself the right to make regulations and impose them on others at will. Only the Sovereign Pontiff, as the successor of Saint Peter, charged by the Divine Redeemer with the feeding of His entire flock, [54] and with him, in obedience to the Apostolic See, the Bishops "whom the Holy Ghost has placed . . . to rule the Church of God," [55] have the right and the duty to govern the Christian people. Consequently, Venerable Brethren, whenever you assert your authority—even on occasion with wholesome severity—you are not merely acquitting yourselves of your duty; you are defending the very will of the Founder of the Church.

PART II
EUCHARISTIC WORSHIP
I. THE NATURE OF THE EUCHARISTIC SACRIFICE

66. The mystery of the Most Holy Eucharist which Christ, the High Priest instituted, and which He commands to be continually renewed in the Church by His Ministers, is the culmination and center, as it were, of the Christian religion. We consider it opportune in speaking about the crowning act of the sacred Liturgy, to delay for a little while and call your attention, Venerable Brethren, to this most important subject.

67. Christ the Lord, "Eternal Priest according to the order of Melchisedech," [56] "loving His own who were in the world," [57] "at the last supper, on the night He was

betrayed, wishing to leave His beloved Spouse, the Church, a visible sacrifice, such as the nature of men requires, that would re-present the bloody Sacrifice offered once on the cross, and perpetuate its memory to the end of time, and whose salutary virtue might be applied in remitting those sins which we daily commit, ... offered His Body and Blood under the species of bread and wine to God the Father, and under the same species allowed the Apostles, whom He at that time constituted the priests of the New Testament, to partake thereof; commanding them and their successors in the priesthood to make the same offering." [58]

It is a true renewal of the Sacrifice of the Cross

68. The august Sacrifice of the altar, then, is no mere empty commemoration of the passion and death of Jesus Christ, but a true and proper act of sacrifice, whereby the High Priest by an unbloody immolation offers Himself a most acceptable Victim to the Eternal Father, as He did upon the Cross. "It is one and the same Victim; the same Person now offers it by the ministry of His Priests, Who then offered Himself on the Cross, the manner of offering alone being different." [59]

a) The same Priest

69. The Priest is the same, Jesus Christ, whose sacred Person His minister represents. Now the minister by reason of the sacerdotal consecration which he has received, is made like to the High Priest and possesses the power of performing actions in virtue of Christ's very Person. [60] Wherefore in his priestly activity he in a certain manner "lends his tongue, and gives his hand" to Christ. [61]

b) The same Victim

70. Likewise the Victim is the same, namely our Divine Redeemer in His human nature with His true Body and Blood. The manner, however, in which Christ is offered is different. On the Cross He completely offered Himself and all His sufferings to God, and the immolation of the Victim was brought about by the bloody death, which He underwent of His free will. But on the altar, by

reason of the glorified state of His human nature, "death shall have no more dominion over Him," [62] and so the shedding of His Blood is impossible; still according to the plan of Divine Wisdom, the Sacrifice of our Redeemer is shown forth in an admirable manner by external signs which are symbols of His death. For by the "transubstantiation" of bread into the Body of Christ and of wine into His Blood, His Body and Blood are both really present: now the Eucharistic species under which He is present, symbolize the actual separation of His Body and Blood. Thus the commemorative representation of His death, which actually took place on Calvary, is repeated in every Sacrifice of the altar, seeing that Jesus Christ is symbolically shown by separate symbols to be in a state of victimhood.

c) The ends of the Sacrifice are the same

71. Moreover, the appointed ends are the same. The first of these is to give glory to the Heavenly Father. From His birth to His death Jesus Christ burned with zeal for the divine glory; and the offering of His Blood upon the Cross rose to heaven in an odor of sweetness. To perpetuate this praise, the members of the Mystical Body are united with their Divine Head in the Eucharistic Sacrifice, and with Him, together with the Angels and Archangels, they sing immortal praise to God [63] and give all honor and glory to the Father Almighty. [64]

72. The second end is duly to give thanks to God. Only the Divine Redeemer, as the Eternal Father's most beloved Son Whose immense love He knew, could offer Him a worthy return of gratitude. This was His intention and desire at the Last Supper when He "gave thanks." [65] He did not cease to do so when hanging upon the Cross, nor does He fail to do so in the august Sacrifice of the altar, which is an act of thanksgiving or a "Eucharistic" act; since this "is truly meet and just, right and availing unto salvation." [66]

73. The third end proposed is that of expiation, propitiation and reconciliation. Certainly no one was better fitted to make satisfaction to Almighty God for all the sins

of men than was Christ. Therefore He desired to be immolated upon the Cross "as a propitiation for our sins, not for ours only but also for those of the whole world." [67] And likewise He daily offers Himself upon our altars for our redemption, that we may be rescued from eternal damnation and admitted into the company of the elect. This He does, not for us only who are in this mortal life, but also "for all who rest in Christ, who have gone before us with the sign of faith and repose in the sleep of peace;" [68] for whether we live, or whether we die "still we are not separated from the one and only Christ." [69]

74. The fourth end, finally, is that of impetration. Man, being the prodigal son, has made bad use of and dissipated the goods which he received from his Heavenly Father. Accordingly, he has been reduced to the utmost poverty and to extreme degradation. However, Christ on the Cross "offering prayers and supplications with a loud cry and tears, has been heard for His reverence." [70] Likewise upon the altar He is our Mediator with God in the same efficacious manner, so that we may be filled with every blessing and grace.

The Infinite Value of the Divine Sacrifice

75. It is easy, therefore, to understand why the holy Council of Trent lays down that by means of the Eucharistic Sacrifice, the saving virtue of the Cross is imparted to us for the remission of the sins we daily commit. [71]

76. Now the Apostle of the Gentiles proclaims the copious plenitude and the perfection of the Sacrifice of the Cross, when he says that Christ by one oblation has perfected for ever them that are sanctified. [72] For the merits of this Sacrifice, since they are altogether boundless and immeasurable, know no limits; for they are meant for all men of every time and place. This follows from the fact that in this Sacrifice the God-Man is the Priest and Victim; that His immolation was entirely perfect, as was His obedience to the will of His Eternal Father; and also that He suffered death as the Head of the human race: "See how we were

bought: Christ hangs upon the Cross, see at what a price He makes His purchase... He sheds His Blood, He buys with His Blood, He buys with the Blood of the Spotless Lamb, He buys with the Blood of God's only Son. He who buys is Christ; the price is His Blood; the possession bought is the world." [73]

77. This purchase, however, does not immediately have its full effect; since Christ after redeeming the world at the lavish cost of His own Blood, still must come into complete possession of the souls of men. Wherefore, that the redemption and salvation of each person and of future generations unto the end of time may be effectively accomplished, and be acceptable to God, it is necessary that men should individually come into vital contact with the Sacrifice of the Cross, so that the merits, which flow from it, should be imparted to them. In a certain sense it can be said that on Calvary Christ built a font of purification and salvation which He filled with the Blood He shed; but if men do not bathe in it and there wash away the stains of their iniquities, they can never be purified and saved.

But the cooperation of the faithful is necessary

78. The cooperation of the faithful is required so that sinners may be individually purified in the Blood of the Lamb. For though, speaking generally, Christ reconciled by His painful death the whole human race with the Father, He wished that all should approach and be drawn to His Cross, especially by means of the Sacraments and the Eucharistic Sacrifice, to obtain the salutary fruits produced by Him upon it. Through this active and individual participation, the members of the Mystical Body not only become daily more like to their divine Head, but the life flowing from the Head is imparted to the members, so that we can each repeat the words of St. Paul: "With Christ I am nailed to the Cross: I live, now not I, but Christ liveth in me." [74] We have already explained sufficiently and of set purpose on another occasion, that Jesus Christ "when dying on the Cross, bestowed upon His Church, as a completely

gratuitous gift, the immense treasure of the Redemption. But when it is a question of distributing this treasure, He not only commits the work of sanctification to His Immaculate Spouse, but also wishes that, to a certain extent, sanctity should derive from her activity." [75]

79. The august Sacrifice of the altar is, as it were, the supreme instrument whereby the merits won by the Divine Redeemer upon the Cross are distributed to the faithful: "as often as this commemorative Sacrifice is offered, there is wrought the work of our Redemption." [76] This, however, so far from lessening the dignity of the actual Sacrifice on Calvary, rather proclaims and renders more manifest its greatness and its necessity, as the Council of Trent declares. [77] Its daily immolation reminds us that there is no salvation except in the Cross of Our Lord Jesus Christ, [78] and that God Himself wishes that there should be a continuation of this Sacrifice "from the rising of the sun till the going down thereof," [79] so that there may be no cessation of the hymn of praise and thanksgiving which man owes to God, seeing that he requires His help continually and has need of the Blood of the Redeemer to remit sin which challenges God's justice.

II. PARTICIPATION OF THE FAITHFUL IN THE EUCHARISTIC SACRIFICE

Participation without priestly power

80. It is therefore desirable, Venerable Brethren, that all the faithful should be aware that to participate in the Eucharistic Sacrifice is their chief duty and supreme dignity, and that not in an inert and negligent fashion, giving way to distractions and daydreaming, but with such earnestness and concentration that they may be united as closely as possible with the High Priest, according to the Apostle: "Let this mind be in you which was also in Christ Jesus." [80] And together with Him and through Him let them make their oblation, and in union with Him let them offer up themselves.

81. It is quite true that Christ is a Priest; but He is a

Priest not for Himself but for us, when in the name of the whole human race He offers our prayers and religious homage to the Eternal Father; He is also a Victim and for us, since He substitutes Himself for sinful man. Now the exhortation of the Apostle: "Let this mind be in you which was also in Christ Jesus," requires that all Christians should possess, as far as is humanly possible, the same dispositions as those which the Divine Redeemer had when He offered Himself in sacrifice: that is to say, they should in a humble attitude of mind, pay adoration, honor, praise and thanksgiving to the supreme Majesty of God. Moreover, it means that they must assume to some extent the character of a victim, that they deny themselves as the Gospel commands, that freely and of their own accord they do penance, and that each detests and satisfies for his sins. It means, in a word, that we must all undergo with Christ a mystical death on the Cross so that we can apply to ourselves the words of St. Paul: "With Christ I am nailed to the Cross." [81]

82. The fact, however, that the faithful participate in the Eucharistic Sacrifice, does not mean that they also are endowed with priestly power. It is very necessary that you make this quite clear to your flocks.

83. For there are today, Venerable Brethren, those who, approximating to errors long since condemned, [82] teach that in the New Testament by the word "priesthood" is meant only that priesthood which applies to all who have been baptized; and hold that the command by which Christ gave power to His Apostles at the Last Supper to do what He Himself had done, applies directly to the entire Christian Church, and that thence, and thence only, arises the hierarchical priesthood. Hence they assert that the people are possessed of a true priestly power, while the priest only acts in virtue of an office committed to him by the community. Wherefore they look on the Eucharistic Sacrifice as a "concelebration," in the literal meaning of that term, and consider it more fitting that priests should "concelebrate" with the people present than that they should offer the Sacrifice privately when the people are absent.

84. It is superfluous to explain how captious errors of this sort completely contradict the truths which we have just stated above, when treating of the place of the priest in the Mystical Body of Jesus Christ. But we deem it necessary to recall that the priest acts for the people only because he represents Jesus Christ, Who is Head of all His members and offers Himself in their stead. Hence he goes to the altar as the minister of Christ, inferior to Christ but superior to the people. [83] The people, on the other hand, since they in no sense represent the Divine Redeemer and are not a mediator between themselves and God, can in no way possess the sacerdotal power.

I—Participation inasmuch as they offer it with the priest

85. All this has the certitude of faith. However, it must also be said that the faithful do offer the Divine Victim, though in a different sense.

a) It is declared by the Church

86. This has already been stated in the clearest terms by some of Our Predecessors and some Doctors of the Church. "Not only," says Innocent III of immortal memory, "do the priests offer the Sacrifice, but also all the faithful: for what the priest does personally by virtue of his ministry, the faithful do collectively by virtue of their intention." [84] We are happy to recall one of St. Robert Bellarmine's many statements on this subject. "The Sacrifice," he says "is principally offered in the person of Christ. Thus the oblation that follows the Consecration, is a sort of attestation that the whole Church consents in the oblation made by Christ, and offers it along with Him." [85]

b) It is signified by the rites themselves

87. Moreover the rites and prayers of the Eucharistic Sacrifice signify and show no less clearly that the oblation of the Victim is made by the priests in company with the people. For not only does the sacred minister, after the oblation of the bread and wine when he turns to the people, say the significant prayer: "Pray Brethren, that my

sacrifice and yours may be acceptable to God the Father Almighty;"[86] but, also the prayers by which the divine Victim is offered to God are generally expressed in the plural number; and in these it is indicated more than once that the people also participate in this august Sacrifice inasmuch as they offer the same. The following words, for example, are used: "For whom we offer, or who offer up to Thee... We therefore beseech Thee, O Lord, to be appeased and to receive this offering of our bounden duty, as also of thy whole household... We thy servants, as also thy whole people... do offer unto thy most excellent majesty, of thine own gifts bestowed upon us, a pure victim, a holy victim, a spotless victim."[87]

88. Nor is it to be wondered at, that the faithful should be raised to this dignity. By the waters of Baptism, as by common right, Christians are made members of the Mystical Body of Christ the Priest, and by the "character" which is imprinted on their souls, they are appointed to give worship to God. Thus they participate, according to their condition, in the priesthood of Christ.

c) The offering of bread and wine made by the people

89. In every age of the Church's history, the mind of man, enlightened by faith, has aimed at the greatest possible knowledge of things divine. It is fitting, then, that the Christian people should also desire to know in what sense they are said in the canon of the Mass to offer up the Sacrifice. To satisfy such a pious desire, then, We shall here explain the matter briefly and concisely.

90. First of all the more extrinsic explanations are these:—it frequently happens that the faithful assisting at Mass join their prayers alternately with those of the priest, and sometimes—a more frequent occurrence in ancient times—they offer to the ministers at the altar bread and wine to be changed into the Body and Blood of Christ, and, finally, by their alms they get the priest to offer the divine Victim for their intentions.

91. But there is also a more profound reason why all Christians, especially those who are present at Mass, are said to offer the Sacrifice.

d) Sacrifice offered by the faithful

92. In this most important subject it is necessary, in order to avoid giving rise to a dangerous error, that we define the exact meaning of the word "offer." The unbloody immolation at the words of consecration, when Christ is made present upon the altar in the state of a victim, is performed by the priest and by him alone, as the representative of Christ and not as the representative of the faithful. It is because the priest places the divine Victim upon the altar that he offers it to God the Father as an oblation for the glory of the Blessed Trinity and for the good of the whole Church. Now the faithful participate in the oblation, understood in this limited sense, after their own fashion and in a twofold manner, namely because they not only offer the Sacrifice by the hands of the priest, but also, to a certain extent, in union with him. It is by reason of this participation, that the offering made by the people is also included in liturgical worship.

93. Now it is clear that the faithful offer the Sacrifice by the hands of the priest from the fact that the minister at the altar in offering a Sacrifice in the name of all His members represents Christ, the Head of the Mystical Body. Hence the whole Church can rightly be said to offer up the Victim through Christ. But the conclusion that the people offer the Sacrifice with the priest himself is not based on the fact that, being members of the Church no less than the priest himself, they perform a visible liturgical rite; for this is the privilege only of the minister who has been divinely appointed to this office: rather, it is based on the fact that the people unite their hearts in praise, impetration, expiation and thanksgiving with the prayers or intention of the priest, even of the High Priest Himself, so that in the one and same offering of the Victim and according to a visible sacerdotal rite, they may be presented to God the Father. It is obviously necessary that the ex-

ternal sacrificial rite should, of its very nature, signify the internal worship of the heart. Now the Sacrifice of the New Law signifies that supreme worship by which the principal Offerer Himself, Who is Christ, and in union with Him and through Him all the members of the Mystical Body, pay God the honor and reverence that are due to Him.

94. We are very pleased to learn that this teaching, thanks to a more intense study of the Liturgy on the part of many, especially in recent years, has been given full recognition. We must, however, deeply deplore certain exaggerations and over-statements which are not in agreement with the true teaching of the Church.

95. Some in fact disapprove altogether of those Masses which are offered privately and without a congregation, on the ground that they are a departure from the ancient way of offering the Sacrifice; moreover, there are some who assert that priests cannot offer Mass at different altars at the same time, because, by doing so, they separate the community of the faithful and imperil its unity; while some go so far as to hold that the people must confirm and ratify the Sacrifice if it is to have its proper force and value.

96. They are mistaken in appealing in this matter to the social character of the Eucharistic Sacrifice, for as often as a priest repeats what the Divine Redeemer did at the Last Supper, the Sacrifice is really completed. Moreover, this Sacrifice, necessarily and of its very nature, has always and everywhere the character of a public and social act, inasmuch as he who offers it, acts in the name of Christ and of the faithful, whose Head is the Divine Redeemer, and he offers it to God for the Holy Catholic Church, and for the living and the dead. [88] This is undoubtedly so, whether the faithful are present—as We desire and commend them to do in great numbers and with devotion—or are not present, since it is in no wise required that the people ratify what the sacred Minister has done.

97. Still, though it is clear from what We have said that the Mass is offered in the name of Christ and of the Church and that it is not robbed of its social effects though

it be celebrated by a priest without a server, nonetheless, on account of the dignity of such an august mystery, it is our earnest desire—as Mother Church has always commanded—that no priest should say Mass unless a server is at hand to answer the prayers, as canon 813 prescribes.

II—Participation inasmuch as they offer themselves as victims

98. In order that the oblation by which the faithful offer the divine Victim in this Sacrifice to the Heavenly Father may have its full effect, it is necessary that the people add something else, namely the offering of themselves as a victim.

99. This offering in fact is not confined merely to the liturgical Sacrifice. For the Prince of the Apostles wishes us, as living stones built upon Christ the corner stone, to be able as "a holy priesthood, to offer up spiritual sacrifices, acceptable to God by Jesus Christ." [89] St. Paul the Apostle addresses the following words of exhortation to Christians, without distinction of time: "I beseech you therefore ... that you present your bodies, a living sacrifice, holy, pleasing unto God, your reasonable service." [90] But at that time especially when the faithful take part in the liturgical service with such piety and recollection that it can truly be said of them: "whose faith and devotion is known to Thee," [91] it is then, with the High Priest and through Him they offer themselves as a spiritual sacrifice, that each one's faith ought to become more ready to work through charity, his piety more real and fervent, and each should consecrate himself to the furthering of the divine glory, desiring to become as like as possible to Christ in His most grievous sufferings.

Purifying their own souls

100. This we are also taught by those exhortations which the Bishop, in the Church's name, addresses to priests on the day of their ordination: "Understand what you do, imitate what you handle, and since you celebrate the mystery of the Lord's death, take good care to mortify

your members with their vices and concupiscences."[92] In almost the same manner the sacred books of the liturgy advise Christians who come to Mass to participate in the Sacrifice: "At this ... altar let innocence be in honor, let pride be sacrificed, anger slain, impurity and every evil desire laid low, let the sacrifice of chastity be offered in place of doves and instead of the young pigeons the sacrifice of innocence."[93] While we stand before the altar, then, it is our duty so to transform our hearts that every trace of sin may be completely blotted out, while whatever promotes supernatural life through Christ, may be zealously fostered and strengthened even to the extent that, in union with the Immaculate Victim, we become a victim acceptable to the Eternal Father.

101. The prescriptions in fact of the sacred Liturgy aim, by every means at their disposal, at helping the Church to bring about this holy purpose in the most suitable manner possible. This is the object not only of readings, homilies and other sermons given by priests, as also the whole cycle of mysteries which are proposed for our commemoration in the course of the year, but it is also the purpose of vestments, of sacred rites and their external splendor. All these things aim at "enhancing the majesty of this great Sacrifice, and raising the minds of the faithful by means of these visible signs of religion and piety, to the contemplation of the sublime truths contained in this Sacrifice."[94]

Reproducing the image of Jesus Christ

102. All the elements of the Liturgy, then, would have us reproduce in our hearts through the mystery of the Cross the likeness of the Divine Redeemer according to the words of the Apostle of the Gentiles: "With Christ I am nailed to the Cross. I live, now not I, but Christ liveth in me."[95] Thus we become a victim, as it were, along with Christ to increase the glory of the Eternal Father.

103. Let this then be the intention and aspiration of the faithful, when they offer up the divine Victim in the Mass. For if, as St. Augustine writes, our mystery is enacted

on the Lord's table, that is Christ our Lord Himself, [96] Who is the Head and symbol of that union through which we are the Body of Christ [97] and members of His Body: [98] if St. Robert Bellarmine teaches, according to the mind of the Doctor of Hippo, that in the Sacrifice of the altar there is signified the general sacrifice by which the whole Mystical Body of Christ, that is all the city of the redeemed, is offered up to God through Christ, the High Priest: [99] nothing can be conceived more just or fitting than that all of us in union with our Head, Who suffered for our sake, should also sacrifice ourselves to the Eternal Father. For in the Sacrament of the altar, as the same St. Augustine has it, the Church is made to see that in what she offers she herself is offered. [100]

104. Let the faithful, therefore, consider to what a high dignity they are raised by the Sacrament of Baptism. They should not think it enough to participate in the Eucharistic Sacrifice with that general intention which befits members of Christ and children of the Church, but let them further, in keeping with the spirit of the Sacred Liturgy, be most closely united with the High Priest and His earthly minister, at the time the consecration of the divine Victim is effected, and at that time especially when those solemn words are pronounced: "By Him and with Him and in Him, is to Thee, God the Father Almighty, in the unity of the Holy Ghost, all honor and glory for ever and ever;" [101] to these words in fact the people answer: "Amen." Nor should Christians forget to offer themselves, their cares, their sorrows, their distress and their necessities in union with their Divine Savior upon the Cross.

III—Means of promoting this participation

105. Therefore they are to be praised who with the idea of getting the Christian people to take part more easily and more fruitfully in the Mass, strive to make them familiar with the "Roman Missal," so that the faithful, united with the priest, may pray together in the very words and sentiments of the Church. They also are to be com-

mended who strive to make the Liturgy even in an external way a sacred act in which all who are present may share. This can be done in more than one way, when, for instance, the whole congregation in accordance with the rules of the Liturgy, either answer the priest in an orderly and fitting manner, or sing hymns suitable to the different parts of the Mass, or do both, or finally in High Masses when they answer the prayers of the minister of Jesus Christ and also sing the liturgical chant.

But subject to the directions of the Church

106. These methods of participation in the Mass are to be approved and commended when they are in complete agreement with the precepts of the Church and the rubrics of the Liturgy. Their chief aim is to foster and promote the people's piety and intimate union with Christ and His visible minister and to arouse those internal sentiments and dispositions which should make our hearts become like to that of the High Priest of the New Testament. However, though they show also in an outward manner that the very nature of the Sacrifice, as offered by the Mediator between God and men, [102] must be regarded as the act of the whole Mystical Body of Christ, still they are by no means necessary to constitute it a public act or to give it a social character. And besides, a "dialogue" Mass of this kind cannot replace the High Mass, which, as a matter of fact, though it should be offered with only the sacred ministers present, possesses its own special dignity due to the impressive character of its ritual and the magnificence of its ceremonies. The splendor and grandeur of a High Mass, however, are very much increased if, as the Church desires, the people are present in great numbers and with devotion.

The value of these methods should not be exaggerated

107. It is to be observed also that they have strayed from the path of truth and right reason who, led away by false opinions, make so much of these accidentals as to pre-

sume to assert that without them the Mass cannot fulfil its appointed end.

108. Many of the faithful are unable to use the "Roman Missal" even though it is written in the vernacular; nor are all capable of understanding correctly the liturgical rites and formulas. So varied and diverse are men's talents and characters that it is impossible for all to be moved and attracted to the same extent by community prayers, hymns, and liturgical services. Moreover, the needs and inclinations of all are not the same, nor are they always constant in the same individual. Who then would say, on account of such a prejudice, that all these Christians cannot participate in the Mass nor share its fruits? On the contrary, they can adopt some other method which proves easier for certain people, for instance, they can lovingly meditate on the mysteries of Jesus Christ or perform other exercises of piety or recite prayers which, though they differ from the sacred rites, are still essentially in harmony with them.

Let diocesan committees be set up to promote the Liturgy

109. Wherefore We exhort you, Venerable Brethren, that each in his Diocese or ecclesiastical jurisdiction supervise and regulate the manner and method in which the people take part in the Liturgy, according to the rubrics of the "Missal" and in keeping with the injunctions which the Sacred Congregation of Rites and the Code of Canon Law have published. Let everything be done with due order and dignity, and let no one, not even a priest, make use of the sacred edifices according to his whim to try out experiments. It is also Our wish that in each Diocese an advisory Committee to promote the liturgical Apostolate should be established, similar to that which cares for sacred music and art, so that with your watchful guidance everything may be carefully carried out in accordance with the prescriptions of the Apostolic See.

110. In religious communities let all those regulations be accurately observed which are laid down in their re-

spective constitutions, nor let any innovations be made which the superiors of these communities have not previously approved.

111. But however much variety and disparity there may be in the exterior manner and circumstances in which the Christian laity participate in the Mass and other liturgical functions, constant and earnest effort must be made to unite the congregation in spirit as much as possible with the Divine Redeemer, so that their lives may be daily enriched with more abundant sanctity, and greater glory be given to the Heavenly Father.

III. HOLY COMMUNION

112. The august Sacrifice of the altar is concluded with Communion or the partaking of the divine feast. But, as all know, the integrity of the Sacrifice only requires that the priest partake of the heavenly Food. Although it is most desirable that the people should also approach the holy table, this is not required for the integrity of the Sacrifice.

For the integrity of the Sacrifice the Communion of the priest is sufficient

113. We wish in this matter to repeat the remarks which Our Predecessor Benedict XIV makes with regard to the definitions of the Council of Trent: "First We must state that none of the faithful can hold that private Masses, in which the priest alone receives Holy Communion, are thereby unlawful and do not fulfil the idea of the true, perfect and complete unbloody Sacrifice instituted by Christ our Lord. For the faithful know quite well, or at least can easily be taught, that the Council of Trent, supported by the doctrine which the uninterrupted tradition of the Church has preserved, condemned the new and false opinion of Luther as opposed to this tradition." [103] "If anyone shall say that Masses in which the priest only receives Communion, are unlawful, and therefore should be abolished, let him be anathema." [104]

114. They therefore err from the path of truth, who do not want to have Masses celebrated unless the faithful communicate; and those are still more in error who, in holding that it is altogether necessary for the faithful to receive Holy Communion as well as the priest, put forward the captious argument that here there is question not of a Sacrifice merely, but of a Sacrifice and a supper of brotherly union, and consider the general Communion of all present as the culminating point of the whole celebration.

115. Now it cannot be over-emphasized that the Eucharistic Sacrifice, of its very nature, is the unbloody immolation of the divine Victim, which is made manifest in a mystical manner by the separation of the Sacred Species and by their oblation to the Eternal Father. Holy Communion pertains to the integrity of the Mass and to the partaking of the august Sacrament; but while it is obligatory for the priest who says the Mass, it is only something earnestly recommended to the faithful.

An exhortation to spiritual and sacramental Communion

116. The Church, as the teacher of truth, strives by every means in her power to safeguard the integrity of the Catholic faith, and like a mother solicitous for the welfare of her children, she exhorts them most earnestly to partake fervently and frequently of the richest treasure of our religion.

117. She wishes in the first place that Christians—especially when they cannot easily receive Holy Communion—should do so at least by desire, so that with renewed faith, reverence, humility and complete trust in the goodness of the Divine Redeemer, they may be united to Him in the spirit of the most ardent charity.

118. But the desire of Mother Church does not stop here. For since by feasting upon the Bread of Angels we can by a "sacramental" Communion, as we have already said, also become partakers of the Sacrifice, she repeats the invitation to all her children individually "Take and

eat ... Do this in memory of Me"[105] so that "we may continually experience within us the fruit of our Redemption"[106] in a more efficacious manner. For this reason the Council of Trent, re-echoing, as it were, the invitation of Christ and His Immaculate Spouse, has earnestly exhorted "the faithful when they attend Mass to communicate not only by a spiritual communion but also by a sacramental one, so that they may obtain more abundant fruit from this most holy Sacrifice."[107] Moreover, our Predecessor of immortal memory, Benedict XIV, wishing to emphasize and throw fuller light upon the truth that the faithful by receiving the Holy Eucharist become partakers of the divine Sacrifice itself, praises the devotion of those who, when attending Mass, not only elicit a desire to receive Holy Communion but also want to be nourished by Hosts consecrated during the Mass, even though, as he himself states, they really and truly take part in the Sacrifice should they receive a Host which has been duly consecrated at a previous Mass. He writes as follows: "And although in addition to those to whom the celebrant gives a portion of the Victim he himself has offered in the Mass, they also participate in the same Sacrifice to whom a priest distributes the Blessed Sacrament that has been reserved; however, the Church has not for this reason ever forbidden, nor does she now forbid, a celebrant to satisfy the piety and just request of those who when present at Mass want to become partakers of the same Sacrifice, because they likewise offer it after their own manner, nay more, she approves of it and desires that it should not be omitted and would reprehend those priests through whose fault and negligence this participation would be denied to the faithful."[108]

For all classes of people

119. May God grant that all accept these invitations of the Church freely and with spontaneity. May He grant that they participate even every day, if possible, in the divine Sacrifice, not only in a spiritual manner, but also by reception of the august Sacrament, receiving the Body of

Jesus Christ which has been offered for all to the Eternal Father. Arouse, Venerable Brethren, in the hearts of those committed to your care, a great and insatiable hunger for Jesus Christ. Under your guidance let the children and youth crowd to the altar rails to offer themselves, their innocence and their works of zeal to the Divine Redeemer. Let husbands and wives approach the holy table so that nourished on this food they may learn to make the children entrusted to them conformed to the mind and heart of Jesus Christ.

120. Let the workers be invited to partake of this sustaining and never failing nourishment that it may renew their strength and obtain for their labors an everlasting recompense in heaven; in a word, invite all men of whatever class and compel them to come in; [109] since this is the Bread of life which all require. The Church of Jesus Christ needs no other bread than this to satisfy fully our souls' wants and desires, and to unite us in the most intimate union with Jesus Christ, to make us "one body," [110] to get us to live together as brothers who, breaking the same bread, sit down to the same Heavenly Table to partake of the elixir of immortality. [111]

Communion to be received if possible during the Mass

121. Now it is very fitting, as the Liturgy otherwise lays down, that the people receive Holy Communion after the priest has partaken of the divine repast upon the altar; and, as we have written above, they should be commended who, when present at Mass, receive Hosts consecrated at the same Mass, so that it is actually verified: "that as many of us as, at this altar, shall partake of and receive the most holy Body and Blood of thy Son, may be filled with every heavenly blessing and grace." [112]

122. Still sometimes there may be a reason, and that not infrequently, why Holy Communion should be distributed before or after Mass and even immediately after the priest receives the Sacred Species—and even though Hosts

consecrated at a previous Mass should be used. In these circumstances,—as we have stated above,—the people duly take part in the Eucharistic Sacrifice and not seldom they can in this way more conveniently receive Holy Communion. Still though the Church with the kind heart of a mother, strives to meet the spiritual needs of her children, they, for their part, should not readily neglect the directions of the Liturgy and, as often as there is no reasonable difficulty should aim that all their actions at the altar manifest more clearly the living unity of the Mystical Body.

Followed by suitable thanksgiving

123. When the Mass, which is subject to special rules of the Liturgy, is over, the person who has received Holy Communion is not thereby freed from his duty of thanksgiving; rather, it is most becoming that, when the Mass is finished, the person who has received the Eucharist should recollect himself, and in intimate union with the Divine Master hold loving and fruitful converse with Him. Hence they have departed from the straight way of truth, who, adhering to the letter rather than the sense, assert and teach that when Mass has ended, no such thanksgiving should be added, not only because the Mass is itself a thanksgiving, but also because this pertains to a private and personal act of piety and not to the good of the community.

124. But, on the contrary, the very nature of the Sacrament demands that its reception should produce rich fruits of Christian sanctity. Admittedly the congregation has been officially dismissed, but each individual, since he is united with Christ, should not interrupt the hymn of praise in his own soul "always returning thanks for all in the name of our Lord Jesus Christ, to God the Father." [113] The sacred Liturgy of the Mass also exhorts us to do this when it bids us pray in these words: "Grant, we beseech thee, that we may always continue to offer thanks[114] . . . and may never cease from praising Thee." [115] Wherefore, if there is no time when we must not offer God thanks, and if we must

never cease from praising Him, who would dare to reprehend or find fault with the Church, because she advises her priests [116] and faithful to converse with the Divine Redeemer for at least a short while after Holy Communion, and inserts in her liturgical books, fitting prayers, enriched with indulgences, by which the sacred ministers may make suitable preparation before Mass and Holy Communion or may return thanks afterwards? So far is the sacred Liturgy from restricting the interior devotion of individual Christians, that it actually fosters and promotes it so that they may be rendered like to Jesus Christ and through Him, be brought to the Heavenly Father; wherefore this same discipline of the Liturgy demands that whoever has partaken of the Sacrifice of the altar, should return fitting thanks to God. For it is the good pleasure of the Divine Redeemer to hearken to us when we pray, to converse with us intimately and to offer us a refuge in His loving Heart.

Necessary to obtain more abundant fruit

125. Moreover such personal colloquies are very necessary that we may all enjoy more fully the supernatural treasures that are contained in the Eucharist and, according to our means, share them with others, so that Christ Our Lord may exert the greatest possible influence on the souls of all.

126. Why then, Venerable Brethren, should We not approve of those who, when they receive Holy Communion, remain on in closest familiarity with their Divine Redeemer even after the congregation has been officially dismissed, and that not only for the consolation of conversing with Him, but also to render Him due thanks and praise and especially to ask help to defend their souls against anything that may lessen the efficacy of the Sacrament and to do everything in their power to cooperate with the action of Christ Who is so intimately present. We exhort them to do so in a special manner by carrying out their resolutions, by exercising the Christian virtues as also by applying to their own necessities the riches they have received with royal liberality. The author of that

golden book *The Imitation of Christ* certainly speaks in accordance with the letter and the spirit of the Liturgy, when he gives the following advice to the person who approaches the altar: "Remain on in secret and take delight in your God; for He is yours Whom the whole world cannot take away from you." [117]

127. Therefore let us all enter into closest union with Christ and strive to lose ourselves, as it were, in His most holy Soul and so be united to Him that we may have a share in those acts with which He adores the Blessed Trinity with a homage that is most acceptable, and by which He offers to the Eternal Father supreme praise and thanks which find an harmonious echo throughout the heavens and the earth, according to the words of the prophet: "All ye works of the Lord, bless the Lord." [118] Finally in union with these sentiments of Christ, let us ask for heavenly aid at that moment that is supremely fitting to pray for and obtain help in His name. [119] For it is especially in virtue of these sentiments that we offer and immolate ourselves as a victim saying: "make of us Thy eternal offering." [120]

128. The Divine Redeemer is ever repeating His pressing invitation: "Abide in Me." [121] Now by the Sacrament of the Eucharist, Christ remains in us and we in Him; and just as Christ, remaining in us, lives and works, so should we remain in Christ and live and work through Him.

IV. ADORATION OF THE EUCHARIST

129. The Eucharistic Food contains, as all are aware, "truly, really and substantially the Body and Blood together with the Soul and Divinity of Our Lord Jesus Christ." [122] It is no wonder, then, that the Church, even from the beginning, adored the Body of Christ under the appearance of bread; this is evident from the very rites of the august Sacrifice, which prescribe that the sacred ministers should adore the Most Holy Sacrament by genuflecting or by profoundly bowing their heads.

130. The Sacred Councils teach that it is the Church's tradition right from the beginning, to worship "with the same adoration the Word Incarnate as well as His own flesh," [123] and St. Augustine asserts that: "No one eats that flesh, without first adoring it," while he adds that "not only do we not commit a sin by adoring it, but that we do sin by not adoring it." [124]

131. It is on this doctrinal basis that the cult of adoring the Eucharist was founded and gradually developed as something distinct from the Sacrifice of the Mass. The reservation of the Sacred Species for the sick and those in danger of death introduced the praiseworthy custom of adoring the Blessed Sacrament which is reserved in our Churches. This practice of adoration, in fact, is based on strong and solid reasons. For the Eucharist is at once a Sacrifice and a Sacrament: but it differs from the other Sacraments in this that it not only produces grace, but contains in a permanent manner the Author of grace Himself. When, therefore, the Church bids us adore Christ hidden behind the Eucharistic veils and pray to Him for spiritual and temporal favors of which we ever stand in need, she manifests living faith in her divine Spouse Who is present beneath these veils, she professes her gratitude to Him and she enjoys the intimacy of His friendship.

Development of the Eucharistic Cult

132. Now, the Church in the course of centuries has introduced various forms of this worship which are ever increasing in beauty and helpfulness; as, for example, visits of devotion to the Tabernacles, even every day, Benediction of the Blessed Sacrament; solemn processions, especially at the time of Eucharistic Congresses, which pass through cities and villages; and adoration of the Blessed Sacrament publicly exposed. Sometimes these public acts of adoration are of short duration. Sometimes they last for one, several and even for forty hours. In certain places they continue in turn in different churches throughout the year,

while elsewhere adoration is perpetual, day and night, under the care of Religious Communities, and the faithful quite often take part in them.

133. These exercises of piety have brought a wonderful increase in faith and supernatural life to the Church militant upon earth and they are re-echoed to a certain extent by the Church triumphant in heaven which sings continually a hymn of praise to God and to the Lamb "Who was slain." [125] Wherefore the Church not merely approves these pious practices which in the course of centuries have spread everywhere throughout the world, but makes them her own, as it were, and by her authority commends them. [126] They spring from the inspiration of the Liturgy and if they are performed with due decorum and with faith and piety, as the liturgical rules of the Church require, they are undoubtedly of the very greatest assistance in living the life of the Liturgy.

No confusion between "the Historic Christ" and "the Eucharistic Christ"

134. Nor is it to be admitted that by this Eucharistic Cult men falsely confound the Historical Christ, as they say, Who once lived on earth, with the Christ Who is present in the august Sacrament of the altar, and Who reigns glorious and triumphant in heaven and bestows supernatural favors. On the contrary, it can be claimed that by this devotion the faithful bear witness to and solemnly avow the faith of the Church that the Word of God is identical with the Son of the Virgin Mary, Who suffered on the Cross, Who is present in a hidden manner in the Eucharist and Who reigns upon His heavenly throne. Thus St. John Chrysostom states: "When you see It (the Body of Christ) exposed, say to yourself: thanks to this Body, I am no longer dust and ashes, I am no more a captive but a freeman: hence I hope to obtain Heaven and the good things that are there in store for me, eternal life, the heritage of the Angels, companionship with Christ; death has not destroyed this Body which was pierced by nails

and scourged, ... this is that Body which was once covered with blood, pierced by a lance, from which issued saving fountains upon the world, one of blood and the other of water ... This Body He gave to us to keep and eat, as a mark of His intense love." [127]

Benediction of the Blessed Sacrament

135. That practice in a special manner is to be highly praised according to which many exercises of piety, customary among the faithful, end with Benediction of the Blessed Sacrament. For excellent and of great benefit is that custom which makes the priest raise aloft the Bread of Angels before congregations with heads bowed down in adoration, and forming with It the sign of the cross implores the Heavenly Father to deign to look upon His Son Who for love of us was nailed to the Cross and for His sake and through Him Who willed to be our Redeemer and our Brother, be pleased to shower down heavenly favors upon those whom the Immaculate Blood of the Lamb has redeemed. [128]

136. Strive then, Venerable Brethren, with your customary devoted care so that the Churches, which the faith and piety of Christian peoples have built in the course of centuries for the purpose of singing a perpetual hymn of glory to God Almighty and of providing a worthy abode for our Redeemer concealed beneath the Eucharistic species, may be entirely at the disposal of greater numbers of the faithful who, called to the feet of their Saviour, hearken to His most consoling invitation: "Come to Me all you who labor and are heavily burdened, and I will refresh you." [129] Let your Churches be the house of God where all who enter to implore blessings rejoice in obtaining whatever they ask [130] and find there heavenly consolation.

137. Only thus can it be brought about that the whole human family settling their differences may find peace, and united in mind and heart may sing this song of hope and charity: "Good Pastor, truly Bread—Jesus have mercy on us—feed us, protect us—bestow on us the vision of all good things—in the land of the living." [131]

PART III
DIVINE OFFICE AND LITURGICAL YEAR
I. THE DIVINE OFFICE

138. The ideal of Christian life is that each one be united to God in the closest and most intimate manner. For this reason, the worship that the Church renders to God, and which is based especially on the Eucharistic Sacrifice and the use of the Sacraments, is directed and arranged in such a way that it embraces, by means of the Divine Office, the hours of the day, the weeks and the whole cycle of the year, and reaches all the aspects and phases of human life.

139. Since the Divine Master commanded "that we ought always to pray and not to faint" [132] the Church faithfully fulfils this injunction and never ceases to pray: she urges us in the words of the Apostle of the Gentiles: "by Him (Jesus) let us offer the sacrifice of praise always to God." [133]

140. Public and common prayer offered to God by all at the same time was customary in antiquity only on certain days and at certain times. Indeed, people prayed to God not only in groups but in private houses and occasionally with neighbors and friends. But soon in different parts of the Christian world the practice arose of setting aside special times for praying, as for example, the last hour of the day when evening set in and the lamps were lighted: or the first, heralded, when the night was coming to an end, by the crowing of the cock and the rising of the morning star. Other times of the day, as being more suitable for prayer are indicated in Sacred Scripture, in Hebrew customs or in keeping with the practice of everyday life. According to the Acts of the Apostles, the disciples of Jesus Christ all came together to pray at the third hour, when they were all filled with the Holy Ghost; [134] and before eating, the Prince of the Apostles went up to the higher parts of the house to pray, about the sixth hour; [135] Peter and John "went up into the Temple at the ninth hour of prayer" [136] and "at midnight Paul and Silas praying... praised God." [137]

141. Thanks to the work of the monks and to those who practiced asceticism, these various prayers in the course of time became ever more perfected and by the authority of the Church were gradually incorporated into the sacred Liturgy.

It is the perennial prayer of the Church

142. The Divine Office is the prayer of the Mystical Body of Jesus Christ, offered to God in the name and on behalf of all Christians, when recited by priests and other ministers of the Church and by religious who are deputed by the Church for this.

143. The character and value of the Divine Office may be gathered from the words recommended by the Church to be said before starting the prayers of the Office, namely that they be said "worthily, with attention and devotion."

144. By assuming human nature, the Divine Word introduced into this earthly exile a hymn which is sung in heaven for all eternity. He unites to Himself the whole human race and with it sings this hymn to the praise of God. As we must humbly recognize that "we know not what we should pray for, as we ought, the Spirit Himself asketh for us with unspeakable groanings." [138] Moreover, through His Spirit in us, Christ entreats the Father. "God could not give a greater gift to men ... (Jesus) prays for us, as our Priest; He prays in us as our Head: we pray to Him as our God ... We recognize in Him our voice and His voice in us ... He is prayed to as God, He prays under the appearance of a servant; in heaven He is Creator, here created though not changed, He assumes a created nature which is to be changed and makes us with Him one complete man, Head and body." [139]

Interior devotion is required

145. To this lofty dignity of the Church's prayer, there should correspond earnest devotion in our souls. For when in prayer the voice repeats those hymns written under the inspiration of the Holy Ghost and extolls God's infinite perfections, it is necessary that the interior senti-

ment of our soul accompany the voice so as to make those sentiments our own in which we are elevated to heaven, adoring and giving due praise and thanks to the Blessed Trinity: "so let us chant in choir that mind and voice may accord together." [140] It is not merely a question of recitation or of singing which, however perfect according to norms of music and the sacred rites, only reaches the ear, but it is especially a question of the ascent of the mind and heart to God so that, united with Christ, we may completely dedicate ourselves and all our actions to Him.

146. On this depends in no small way the efficacy of our prayers. These prayers in fact when they are not addressed directly to the Word made man, conclude with the phrase "through Jesus Christ Our Lord." As our Mediator with God, He shows to the heavenly Father His glorified wounds, "always living to make intercession for us." [141]

The wonderful content of the Psalter

147. The Psalms, as all know, form the chief part of the Divine Office. They encompass the full round of the day and sanctify it. Cassidorus speaks beautifully about the Psalms as distributed in his day throughout the Divine Office: "with the celebration of matins they bring a blessing on the coming day, they set aside for us the first hour and consecrate the third hour of the day, they gladden the sixth hour with the breaking of bread, at the ninth they terminate our fast, they bring the evening to a close and at nightfall they shield our minds from darkness." [142]

148. The Psalms recall to mind the truths revealed by God to the chosen people, which were at one time frightening and at another filled with wonderful tenderness: they keep repeating and fostering the hope of the promised Liberator which in ancient times was kept alive with song, either around the hearth or in the stately Temple; they show forth in splendid light the prophesied glory of Jesus Christ: first, His supreme and eternal power, then His lowly coming to this terrestrial exile, His kingly dignity and priestly power and finally his beneficent labors, and the

shedding of His Blood for our redemption. In a similar way they express the joy, the bitterness, the hope and fear of our hearts and our desire of loving God and hoping in Him alone, and our mystic ascent to divine tabernacles.

149. "The psalm is ... a blessing for the people, it is the praise of God, the tribute of the nation, the common language and acclamation of all, it is the voice of the Church, the harmonious confession of faith, signifying deep attachment to authority: it is the joy of freedom, the expression of happiness, an echo of bliss." [143]

The participation of the faithful in Sunday Vespers

150. In an earlier age, these canonical prayers were attended by many of the faithful: but this gradually ceased, and, as We have already said, their recitation at present is the duty only of the clergy and of religious. The laity have no obligation in this matter. Still, it is greatly to be desired that they participate in reciting or chanting Vespers sung in their own parish on feast-days. We earnestly exhort you, Venerable Brethren, to see that this pious practice is kept up, and that wherever it has ceased you restore it if possible. This, without doubt, will produce salutary results when Vespers are conducted in a worthy and fitting manner and with such helps as foster the piety of the faithful. Let the public and private observance of the feasts of the Church, which are in a special way dedicated and consecrated to God, be kept inviolable: and especially the Lord's day which the Apostles under the guidance of the Holy Ghost, substituted for the Sabbath. Now, if the order was given to the Jews: "Six days shall you do work: in the seventh day is the sabbath, the rest holy to the Lord. Every one that shall do any work on this day, shall die:" [144] how will these Christians not fear spiritual death, who perform servile work on feast-days, and whose rest on these days is not devoted to religion and piety but given over to the allurements of the world? Sundays and Holydays, then, must be made holy by divine worship, which gives homage

to God and heavenly food to the soul. Although the Church only commands the faithful to abstain from servile work and attend Mass and does not make it obligatory to attend evening devotions, still she desires this and recommends it repeatedly: moreover, the needs of each one demand it, seeing that all are bound to win the favor of God if they are to obtain His benefits. Our Soul is filled with the greatest grief when We see how the Christian people of today profane the afternoon of feast-days: public places of amusement and public games are frequented in great numbers while the Churches are not as full as they should be. All should come to our Churches and there be taught the truth of the Catholic faith, sing the praises of God, be enriched with Benediction of the Blessed Sacrament given by the priest, and be strengthened with help from heaven against the adversities of this life. Let all try to learn those prayers which are recited at Vespers and fill their souls with their meaning. When deeply penetrated by these prayers they will experience what St. Augustine said about himself: "How much did I weep during hymns and verses, greatly moved at the sweet singing of thy Church. Their sound would penetrate my ears and their truth melt my heart, sentiments of piety would well up, tears would flow and that was good for me." [145]

II. THE CYCLE OF THE MYSTERIES IN THE LITURGICAL YEAR

151. Throughout the entire year, the Mass and the Divine Office center especially around the person of Jesus Christ: this arrangement is so suitably disposed that Our Saviour dominates the scene in the mysteries of His humiliation, of His redemption and triumph.

152. While the sacred Liturgy calls to mind the mysteries of Jesus Christ, it strives to make all believers take their part in them so that the divine Head of the Mystical Body may live in all the members with the fulness of His holiness. Let the souls of Christians be like altars on each one of which a different phase of the Sacrifice, offered by

the High Priest, comes to life again, as it were:—pains and tears which wipe away and expiate sin; supplication to God which pierces heaven; dedication and even immolation of oneself made promptly, generously and earnestly; and finally that intimate union by which we commit ourselves and all we have to God, in Whom we find our rest; "the perfection of religion is to imitate whom you adore." [146]

The significance of the Liturgical Season

153. By these suitable ways and methods in which the Liturgy at stated times proposes the life of Jesus Christ for our meditation, the Church gives us examples to imitate, points out treasures of sanctity for us to make our own; since it is fitting that the mind believes what the lips sing, and that what the mind believes should be practised in public and private life.

Advent

154. In the period of Advent, for instance, the Church arouses in us the consciousness of the sins we have had the misfortune to commit, and urges us, by restraining our desires and practicing voluntary mortification of the body, to recollect ourselves in meditation, and experience a longing desire to return to God Who alone can free us by His grace from the stain of sin and from its evil consequences.

Christmas

155. With the coming of the birthday of the Redeemer, she would bring us to the cave of Bethlehem and there teach that we must be born again and undergo a complete reformation; that will only happen when we are intimately and vitally united to the Word of God made man and participate in His divine nature, to which we have been elevated.

Epiphany

156. At the solemnity of the Epiphany, in putting before us the call of the gentiles to the Christian faith, she wishes us daily to give thanks to the Lord for such a blessing; she wishes us to seek with lively faith the living and

true God, to penetrate deeply and religiously the things of heaven, to love silence and meditation in order to perceive and grasp more easily heavenly gifts.

Septuagesima

157. During the days of Septuagesima and Lent, Our Holy Mother the Church over and over again strives to make each of us seriously consider our misery, so that we may be urged to a practical emendation of our lives, detest our sins heartily and expiate them by prayer and penance. For constant prayer and penance done for past sins obtain for us divine help, without which every work of ours is useless and unavailing.

Holy Week

158. In Holy Week, when the most bitter sufferings of Jesus Christ are put before us by the Liturgy, the Church invites us to come to Calvary and follow in the bloodstained footsteps of the Divine Redeemer, to carry the cross willingly with Him, to reproduce in our own hearts His spirit of expiation and atonement, and to die together with Him.

Easter

159. At the Paschal Season, which commemorates the triumph of Christ, our souls are filled with deep interior joy: we, accordingly, should also consider that we must rise, in union with the Redeemer, from our cold and slothful life to one of greater fervor and holiness by giving ourselves completely and generously to God, and by forgetting this wretched world in order to aspire only to the things of heaven: "if you be risen with Christ, seek the things that are above ... mind the things that are above." [147]

Pentecost

160. Finally, during the time of Pentecost, the Church by precept and practice urges us to be more docile to the action of the Holy Spirit Who wishes us to be on fire with divine love so that we may daily strive to advance more in virtue and thus become holy as Christ Our Lord and His Father are holy.

161. Thus, the Liturgical Year should be considered as a splendid hymn of praise offered to the Heavenly Father by the Christian family through Jesus their perpetual Mediator. Nevertheless, it requires a diligent and well-ordered study on our part to be able to know and praise Our Redeemer ever more and more: it requires a serious effort and constant practice to imitate His mysteries, to enter willingly upon His path of sorrow and thus finally share His glory and eternal happiness.

Errors of modern authors

162. From what We have already explained, Venerable Brethren, it is perfectly clear how much modern writers are wanting in the genuine and true Liturgical spirit who, deceived by the illusion of a higher mysticism, dare to assert that attention should be paid not to the historic Christ but to a "pneumatic" or glorified Christ. They do not hesitate to assert that a change has taken place in the piety of the faithful by dethroning, as it were, Christ from His position; since they say that the glorified Christ, Who liveth and reigneth forever and sitteth at the right hand of the Father, has been overshadowed and in His place has been substituted that Christ Who lived on earth. For this reason, some have gone so far as to want to remove from the Churches images of the Divine Redeemer suffering on the cross.

163. But these false statements are completely opposed to the solid doctrine handed down by tradition. "You believe in Christ born in the flesh," says St. Augustine, "and you will come to Christ begotten of God." [148] In the sacred Liturgy, the whole Christ is proposed to us in all the circumstances of His life, as the Word of the Eternal Father, as born of the Virgin Mother of God, as He Who teaches us truth, heals the sick, consoles the afflicted, Who endures suffering and Who dies; finally, as He Who rose triumphantly from the dead and Who, reigning in the glory of heaven sends us the Holy Paraclete and Who abides in His Church forever": "Jesus Christ, yesterday and today; and

the same forever." [149] Besides, the Liturgy shows us Christ not only as a Model to be imitated but as a Master to Whom we should listen readily, a Shepherd Whom we should follow, Author of our salvation, the Source of our holiness and the Head of the Mystical Body whose members we are, living by His very life.

164. Since His bitter sufferings constitute the principal mystery of our Redemption it is only fitting that the Catholic faith should give it the greatest prominence. This mystery is the very center of divine worship since the Mass represents and renews it every day and since all the Sacraments are most closely united with the Cross. [150]

Christ lives again in the Church during the Liturgical Year

165. Hence the Liturgical Year devotedly fostered and accompanied by the Church, is not a cold and lifeless representation of the events of the past, or a simple and bare record of a former age. It is rather Christ Himself Who is ever living in His Church. Here He continues that journey of immense mercy which He lovingly began in His mortal life, going about doing good [151] with the design of bringing men to know His mysteries and in a way live by them. These mysteries are ever present and active not in a vague and uncertain way as some modern writers hold, but in the way that Catholic doctrine teaches us. According to the Doctors of the Church, they are shining examples of Christian perfection, as well as sources of divine grace, due to the merit and prayers of Christ; they still influence us because each mystery brings its own special grace for our salvation. Moreover, our holy Mother the Church, while proposing for our contemplation the mysteries of our Redeemer, asks in her prayers for those gifts which would give her children the greatest possible share in the spirit of these mysteries through the merits of Christ. By means of His inspiration and help and through the cooperation of our wills we can receive from Him living vitality as branches do from the tree and members from

the head; thus slowly and laboriously we can transform ourselves "unto the measure of the age of the fulness of Christ." [152]

III. FEASTS OF THE SAINTS

166. In the course of the Liturgical Year besides the mysteries of Jesus Christ, the feasts of the Saints are celebrated. Even though these feasts are of a lower and subordinate order, the Church always strives to put before the faithful examples of sanctity in order to move them to cultivate in themselves the virtues of the Divine Redeemer.

Examples proposed to us

167. We should imitate the virtues of the Saints just as they imitated Christ, for in their virtues there shines forth under different aspects the splendor of Jesus Christ. Among some of the saints the zeal of the apostolate stood out, in others courage prevailed even to the shedding of blood, constant vigilance marked others out as they kept watch for the Divine Redeemer, while in others the virginal purity of soul was resplendent and their modesty revealed the beauty of Christian humility: there burned in all of them the fire of charity towards God and their neighbor. The sacred Liturgy puts all these gems of sanctity before us so that we may consider them for our salvation, and "rejoicing at their merits, we may be inflamed by their example." [153] It is necessary then to practice "in simplicity innocence, in charity concord, in humility modesty, diligence in government, readiness in helping those who labor, mercy in serving the poor, in defending truth constancy, in the strict maintenance of discipline justice, so that nothing may be wanting in us of the virtues which have been proposed for our imitation. These are the footprints left by the Saints in their journey homeward, that guided by them we might follow them into glory." [154] In order that we may be helped by our senses also, the Church wishes that images of the Saints be displayed in our Churches, always, however, with the same intention "that we imitate the virtues of those whose images we venerate." [155]

And as our intercessors

168. But there is another reason why the Christian people should honor the Saints in heaven, namely, to implore their help and "that we be aided by the pleadings of those whose praise is our delight." [156] Hence, it is easy to understand why the sacred Liturgy provides us with many different prayers to invoke the intercession of the Saints.

Pre-eminent devotion to Mary Most Holy

169. Among the Saints in heaven the Virgin Mary Mother of God is venerated in a special way. Because of the mission she received from God, her life is most closely linked with the mysteries of Jesus Christ, and there is no one who has followed in the footsteps of the Incarnate Word more closely and with more merit than she: and no one has more grace and power over the Most Sacred Heart of the Son of God and through Him with the Heavenly Father. Holier than the Cherubim and Seraphim, she enjoys unquestionably greater glory than all the other Saints, for she is "full of grace," [157] she is the Mother of God, who happily gave birth to the Redeemer for us. Since she is, therefore, "Mother of mercy, our life, our sweetness and our hope" let us all cry to her "mourning and weeping in this vale of tears," [158] and confidently place ourselves and all we have under her patronage. She became our Mother also when the Divine Redeemer offered the Sacrifice of Himself; and hence by this title also, we are her children. She teaches us all the virtues; she gives us her Son and with Him all the help we need, for God "wished us to have everything through Mary." [159]

170. Throughout this liturgical journey which begins anew for us each year under the sanctifying action of the Church, and strengthened by the help and example of the Saints, especially of the Immaculate Virgin Mary, "let us draw near with a true heart, in fulness of faith having our hearts sprinkled from an evil conscience, and our bodies washed with clean water" [160] let us draw near to the "High Priest" [161] that with Him we may share His life and sen-

timents and by Him penetrate "even within the veil," [162] and there honor the Heavenly Father for ever and ever.

171. Such is the nature and the object of the sacred Liturgy: it treats of the Mass, the Sacraments, the Divine Office; it aims at uniting our souls with Christ and sanctifying them through the Divine Redeemer in order that Christ be honored and, through Him and in Him, the Most Holy Trinity: *Glory be to the Father and to the Son and to the Holy Ghost.*

PART IV
PASTORAL DIRECTIVES
I. OTHER DEVOTIONS NOT STRICTLY LITURGICAL WARMLY RECOMMENDED

172. In order that the errors and inaccuracies, mentioned above, may be more easily removed from the Church, and that the faithful following safer norms may be able to use more fruitfully the liturgical apostolate, We have deemed it opportune, Venerable Brethren, to add some practical applications of the doctrine which We have explained.

173. When dealing with genuine and solid piety We stated that there could be no real opposition between the sacred Liturgy and other religious practices, provided they be kept within legitimate bounds and performed for a legitimate purpose. In fact, there are certain exercises of piety which the Church recommends very much to clergy and religious.

174. It is Our wish also that the faithful, as well, should take part in these practices. The chief of these are: meditation on spiritual things, diligent examination of conscience, enclosed retreats, visits to the Blessed Sacrament, and those special prayers in honor of the Blessed Virgin Mary among which the rosary, as all know, has pride of place. [163]

The action of the Holy Spirit is not foreign to these devotions

175. From these multiple forms of piety, the inspiration and action of the Holy Spirit cannot be absent. Their

purpose is, in various ways, to attract and direct our souls to God, purifying them from their sins, encouraging them to practice virtue and finally stimulating them to advance along the path of sincere piety by accustoming them to meditate on the eternal truths and disposing them better to contemplate the mysteries of the divine and human nature of Christ. Besides, since they develop a deeper spiritual life in the faithful, they prepare them to take part in sacred public functions with greater fruit, and they lessen the danger of liturgical prayers becoming an empty ritualism.

Errors from which the faithful should be protected

176. In keeping with your pastoral solicitude, Venerable Brethren, do not cease to recommend and encourage these exercises of piety from which the faithful, entrusted to your care, cannot but derive salutary fruit. Above all, do not allow—as some do, who are deceived under the pretext of restoring the Liturgy or who idly claim that only liturgical rites are of any real value and dignity—that Churches be closed during the hours not appointed for public functions, as has already happened in some places: where the adoration of the august Sacrament and visits to Our Lord in the tabernacles are neglected: where confession of devotion is discouraged: and devotion to the Virgin Mother of God, a sign of "predestination" according to the opinion of holy men, is so neglected, especially among the young, as to fade away and gradually vanish. Such conduct most harmful to Christian piety is like poisonous fruit, growing on the infected branches of a healthy tree, which must be cut off so that the life-giving sap of the tree may bring forth only the best fruit.

Sacramental Confession

177. Since the opinions expressed by some about frequent confession, are completely foreign to the spirit of Christ and His Immaculate Spouse and are most dangerous to the spiritual life, let Us call to mind what with sorrow We wrote about this point in the Encyclical on the Mystical

Body; We urgently insist once more that what We expounded in very serious words, be proposed by you for the serious consideration and dutiful obedience of your flock, especially to students for the priesthood and young clergy.

Spiritual Exercises and Retreats

178. Take special care that as many as possible, not only of the clergy but of the laity and especially those in religious organizations and in the ranks of Catholic Action, take part in monthly days of recollection and in retreats of longer duration, made with a view to growing in virtue. As We have previously stated, such spiritual exercises are most useful and even necessary to instill into souls solid virtue, and to strengthen them in sanctity so as to be able to derive from the sacred Liturgy more efficacious and abundant benefits.

179. As regards the different methods employed in these exercises, it is perfectly clear to all that in the Church on earth, no less than in the Church in heaven, there are many mansions; [164] and that asceticism cannot be the monopoly of anyone. It is the same Spirit Who breatheth where He will; [165] and Who with differing gifts and in different ways enlightens and guides souls to sanctity. Let their freedom and the supernatural action of the Holy Spirit be so sacrosanct that no one will presume to disturb or stifle them for any reason whatsoever.

180. However, it is well known that the spiritual exercises according to the method and norms of St. Ignatius have been fully approved and earnestly recommended by Our Predecessors on account of their admirable efficacy. We, too, for the same reason have approved and commended them and willingly do We repeat this now.

181. Any inspiration to follow and practice extraordinary exercises of piety must most certainly come from the Father of Lights, from Whom every good and perfect gift descends; [166] and of course the criterion of this will be the effectiveness of these exercises in making the divine cult loved and spread daily ever more widely, and in making

the faithful approach the Sacraments with more longing desire, and in obtaining for all things holy due respect and honor. If, on the contrary, they are an obstacle to the principles and norms of divine worship, or if they oppose or hinder them, one must surely conclude that they are not in keeping with prudence and enlightened zeal.

Other practices not strictly liturgical

182. There are, besides, other exercises of piety which although not strictly belonging to the sacred Liturgy are, nevertheless, of special import and dignity, and may be considered in a certain way to be an addition to the liturgical cult: they have been approved and praised over and over again by the Apostolic See and by the Bishops. Among these are the prayers usually said during the month of May in honor of the Blessed Virgin Mother of God, or during the month of June to the Most Sacred Heart of Jesus; also Novenas and Triduums, Stations of the Cross and other similar practices.

183. These devotions make us partakers in a salutary manner of the liturgical cult, because they urge the faithful to go frequently to the Sacrament of Penance, to attend Mass and receive Communion with devotion, and, as well, encourage them to meditate on the mysteries of our Redemption and imitate the example of the Saints.

184. Hence he would do something very wrong and dangerous, who would dare to take on himself to reform all these exercises of piety and reduce them completely to the methods and norms of liturgical rites. However, it is necessary that the spirit of the sacred Liturgy and its directives should exercise such a salutary influence on them that nothing improper be introduced nor anything unworthy of the dignity of the House of God or detrimental to the sacred functions or opposed to solid piety.

185. Take care then, Venerable Brethren, that this true and solid piety increases daily more and more under your guidance and bears more abundant fruit. Above all, do not cease to inculcate into the minds of all that progress in the

Christian life does not consist in the multiplicity and variety of prayers and exercises of piety, but rather in their helpfulness towards spiritual progress of the faithful and constant growth of the Church universal. For the Eternal Father "chose us in Him, (Christ) before the foundation of the world that we should be holy and unspotted in His sight." [167] All our prayers, then, and all our religious practices should aim at directing our spiritual energies towards attaining this most noble and lofty end.

II. LITURGICAL SPIRIT AND LITURGICAL APOSTOLATE

186. We earnestly exhort you, Venerable Brethren, that after errors and falsehoods have been removed, and anything that is contrary to truth or moderation has been condemned, you promote a deeper knowledge among the people of the sacred Liturgy so that they more readily and easily follow the sacred rites and take part in them with true Christian dispositions.

Obedience to the directions of the Church

187. First of all, you must strive that with due reverence and faith all obey the decrees of the Council of Trent, of the Roman Pontiffs, and the Sacred Congregation of Rites, and what the liturgical books ordain concerning external public worship.

188. Three characteristics, of which Our Predecessor Pius X spoke, should adorn all liturgical services:—sacredness, which abhors any profane influence; nobility, which true and genuine arts should serve and foster; and universality, which while safeguarding local and legitimate custom, reveals the Catholic unity of the Church. [168]

The adornment of Churches and altars

189. We desire to commend and urge the adornment of Churches and altars. Let each one feel moved by the inspired word: "the zeal of thy house hath eaten me up"; [169] and strive as much as in him lies, that everything in the Church, including vestments and liturgical furnishings, even though not rich nor lavish, be perfectly clean

and appropriate, since all is consecrated to the Divine Majesty. If We have previously disapproved of the error of those who would wish to outlaw images from Churches on the plea of reviving an ancient tradition, We now deem it Our duty to censure the inconsiderate zeal of those who propose for veneration in the Churches and on the altars, without any just reason, a multitude of sacred images and statues, and also those who display unauthorized relics, those who emphasize special and insignificant practices, neglecting essential and necessary things; they thus bring religion into derision and lessen the dignity of worship.

190. Let us recall, as well, the decree about "not introducing new forms of worship and devotion." [170] We commend the exact observance of this decree to your vigilance.

191. As regards music, let the clear and guiding norms of the Apostolic See be scrupulously observed. Gregorian chant, which the Roman Church considers her own as handed down from antiquity and kept under her close tutelage, is proposed to the faithful as belonging to them also. In certain parts of the Liturgy the Church definitely prescribes it; [171] it makes the celebration of the Sacred Mysteries not only more dignified and solemn but helps very much to increase the faith and devotion of the congregation. For this reason, Our Predecessors of immortal memory, Pius X and Pius XI, decreed—and We are happy to confirm with Our authority the norms laid down by them—that in Seminaries and Religious Institutes, Gregorian chant be diligently and zealously promoted, and moreover that the old "*Scholae Cantorum*" be restored, at least in the principal Churches; this has already been done with happy results in not a few places. [172]

Gregorian chant and congregational singing

192. Besides, "so that the faithful may take a more active part in divine worship, let Gregorian chant be restored to popular use in the parts proper to the people. Indeed it is

very necessary that the faithful attend the sacred ceremonies not as if they were outsiders or mute onlookers, but let them fully appreciate the beauty of the Liturgy and take part in the sacred ceremonies, alternating their voices with the priest and the choir, according to the prescribed norms. If, please God, this is done, it will not happen that the congregation hardly ever or only in a low murmur answer the prayers in Latin or in the vernacular." [173] A congregation that is devoutly present at the Sacrifice, in which Our Saviour together with His children redeemed with His Sacred Blood sings the nuptial hymn of His immense love, cannot keep silent, for "song befits the lover" [174] and, as the ancient saying has it, "he who sings well prays twice." Thus the Church militant, faithful as well as clergy, joins in the hymns of the Church triumphant and with the choirs of Angels, and, all together, sing a wondrous and eternal hymn of praise to the most Holy Trinity in keeping with words of the Preface: "with whom our voices too, thou wouldst bid to be admitted." [175]

193. It cannot be said that modern music and singing should be entirely excluded from Catholic worship. For, if they are not profane nor unbecoming to the sacredness of the place and function, and do not spring from a desire of achieving extraordinary and unusual effects, then our Churches must admit them since they can contribute in no small way to the splendor of the sacred ceremonies, can lift the mind to higher things and foster true devotion of soul.

194. We also exhort you, Venerable Brethren, to promote with care congregational singing, and to see to its accurate execution with all due dignity, since it easily stirs up and arouses the faith and piety of large gatherings of the faithful. Let the full harmonious singing of our people rise to heaven like the bursting of a thunderous sea [176] and let them testify by the melody of their song to the unity of their hearts and minds, [177] as becomes brothers and the children of the same Father.

The other arts in the liturgical cult

195. What We have said about music, applies to the other fine arts, especially to architecture, sculpture and painting. Recent works of art which lend themselves to the materials of modern composition, should not be universally despised and rejected through prejudice. Modern art should be given free scope in the due and reverent service of the Church and the sacred rites, provided that they preserve a correct balance between styles tending neither to extreme realism nor to excessive "symbolism," and that the needs of the Christian community are taken into consideration rather than the particular taste or talent of the individual artist. Thus modern art will be able to join its voice to that wonderful choir of praise to which have contributed, in honor of the Catholic faith, the greatest artists throughout the centuries. Nevertheless, in keeping with the duty of Our office, We cannot help deploring and condemning those works of art, recently introduced by some, which seem to be a distortion and perversion of true art and which at times openly shock Christian taste, modesty and devotion, and shamefully offend the true religious sense: these must be entirely excluded and banished from our Churches, like "anything else that is not in keeping with the sanctity of the place." [178]

196. Keeping in mind, Venerable Brethren, Pontifical norms and decrees, take great care to enlighten and direct the minds and hearts of the artists to whom is given the task today of restoring or rebuilding the many Churches which have been ruined or completely destroyed by war: let them be capable and willing to draw their inspiration from religion to express what is suitable and more in keeping with the requirements of worship. Thus the human arts will happily shine forth with a wondrous heavenly splendor, and contribute greatly to human civilization, to the salvation of souls and the glory of God. The fine arts are really in conformity with religion when "as noblest handmaids they are at the service of divine worship." [179]

Important that clergy and people live the liturgical life

197. But there is something else of even greater importance, Venerable Brethren, which We commend to your apostolic zeal, in a very special manner. Whatever pertains to the external worship has assuredly its importance; however, the most pressing duty of Christians is to live the liturgical life, and increase and cherish its supernatural spirit.

198. Readily provide the young clerical student with facilities to understand the sacred ceremonies, to appreciate their majesty and beauty and to learn the rubrics with care, just as you do when he is trained in ascetics, in dogma and in canon law and pastoral theology. This should not be done merely for cultural reasons and to fit the student to perform religious rites in the future, correctly and with due dignity, but especially to lead him into closest union with Christ the Priest so that he may become a holy minister of sanctity.

199. Try in every way, with the means and helps that your prudence deems best, that the clergy and people become one in mind and heart, and that the Christian people take such an active part in the Liturgy that it becomes a truly sacred action of due worship to the Eternal Lord in which the priest, chiefly responsible for the souls of his parish, and the ordinary faithful are united together.

Altar boys in the service of the altar

200. To attain this purpose, it will greatly help to select carefully good and upright young boys from all classes of citizens who will come generously and spontaneously to serve at the altar with careful zeal and exactness. Parents of higher social standing and culture should greatly esteem this office for their children. If these youths, under the watchful guidance of the priests, are properly trained and encouraged to fulfil the task committed to them punctually, reverently and constantly, then from their number will readily come fresh candidates for the priesthood. The clergy

will not then complain—as, alas sometimes happens even in Catholic places—that in the celebration of the august Sacrifice they find no one to answer or serve them.

Pastoral Zeal

201. Above all, try with your constant zeal to have all the faithful attend the Eucharistic Sacrifice from which they may obtain abundant and salutary fruit; and carefully instruct them in all the legitimate ways We have described above so that they may devoutly participate in it. The Mass is the chief act of divine worship; it should also be the source and center of Christian piety. Never think that you have satisfied your apostolic zeal until you see your faithful approach in great numbers the celestial banquet which is a sacrament of devotion, a sign of unity and a bond of love. [180]

202. By means of suitable sermons and particularly by periodic conferences and lectures, by special study weeks and the like, teach the Christian people carefully about the treasures of piety contained in the sacred Liturgy so that they may be able to profit more abundantly by these supernatural gifts. In this matter, those who are active in the ranks of Catholic Action will certainly be a help to you, since they are ever at the service of the Hierarchy in the work of promoting the Kingdom of Jesus Christ.

Vigilance against errors and prejudices

203. But in all these matters, it is essential that you watch vigilantly lest the enemy come into the field of the Lord and sow cockle among the wheat; [181] in other words, do not let your flocks be deceived by the subtle and dangerous errors of false mysticism or quietism—as you know We have already condemned these errors;— [182] also do not let a certain dangerous "humanism" lead them astray, nor let there be introduced a false doctrine destroying the notion of Catholic faith, nor finally an exaggerated zeal for antiquity in matters liturgical. Watch with like diligence lest the false teaching of those be propagated, who

wrongly think and teach that the glorified human nature of Christ really and continually dwells in the "just," by His presence and that one and numerically the same grace, as they say, unites Christ with the members of His Mystical Body.

204. Never be discouraged by the difficulties that arise, and never let your pastoral zeal grow cold. "Blow the trumpet in Sion ... call an assembly, gather together the people, sanctify the Church, assemble the ancients, gather together the little ones and them that suck at the breasts," [183] and use every help to get the faithful everywhere to fill the Churches and crowd around the altars so that they may be restored by the graces of the Sacraments and joined as living members to their divine Head, and with Him and through Him celebrate together the august Sacrifice that gives due tribute of praise to the Eternal Father.

EPILOGUE

205. These, Venerable Brethren, are the subjects We desired to write to you about. We are moved to write that your children, who are also Ours, may more fully understand and appreciate the most precious treasures which are contained in the sacred Liturgy: namely, the Eucharistic Sacrifice, representing and renewing the Sacrifice of the Cross, the Sacraments, which are the streams of divine grace and of divine life, and the hymn of praise, which heaven and earth daily offer to God.

206. We cherish the hope that these Our exhortations will not only arouse the sluggish and recalcitrant to a deeper and more correct study of the Liturgy, but will also instill into their daily lives its supernatural spirit according to the words of the Apostle: "extinguish not the spirit." [184]

207. To those whom an excessive zeal occasionally led to say and do certain things which saddened Us and which We could not approve We repeat the warning of St. Paul: "But prove all things, hold fast that which is good"; [185] let Us paternally warn them to imitate in their thoughts and

actions the Christian doctrine which is in harmony with the precepts of the Immaculate Spouse of Jesus Christ, the Mother of Saints.

208. Let Us remind all that they must generously and faithfully obey their holy Pastors who possess the right and duty of regulating the whole life, especially the spiritual life, of the Church: "Obey your prelates and be subject to them. For they watch as having to render an account of your souls; that they may do this with joy and not with grief." [186]

209. May God, Whom we worship, and Who is "not the God of dissension but of peace," [187] graciously grant to us all that during our earthly exile we may with one mind and one heart participate in the sacred Liturgy which is, as it were, a preparation and a token of that heavenly Liturgy in which we hope one day to sing together with the most glorious Mother of God and our most loving Mother: "To Him that sitteth on the throne, and to the Lamb, benediction and honor, and glory and power for ever and ever." [188]

210. In this joyous hope, We most lovingly impart to each and every one of you, Venerable Brethren, and to the flocks confided to your care, as a pledge of divine gifts and as a witness of Our special love, the Apostolic Benediction.

211. Given at Castel Gandolfo, near Rome, on the 20th day of November in the year 1947, the 9th of Our Pontificate.   PIUS PP. XII

FOOTNOTES

[1] 1 *Tim.*, 2:5.   [2] Cf. *Hebr.*, 4:14.
[3] Cf. *Hebr.*, 9:14.   [4] Cf. *Mal.*, 1:2.
[5] Cf. Conc. Trid., Sess. XXII, c. 1.   [6] Cf. *Ibid.*, c. 2
[7] Litt. Encycl. *Caritate Christi* d. d. III Maii a. MCMXXXII.
[8] Cf. Litt. Ap. Motu Proprio *In cotidianis precibus* d. d. XXIV Martii a. MCMXXXXV.   [9] 1 *Cor.*, 10:17.
[10] S. Thom., *Summa Theol.*, II-II, q. LXXXI, art. 1.
[11] Cf. Lib. *Levitici.*   [12] Cf. *Hebr.*, 10:1.   [13] *Ioan.*, 1:14.
[14] *Hebr.*, 10:5-7.   [15] *Ibidem*, 10:10.   [16] *Ioan.*, 1:9.
[17] *Hebr.*, 10:39.   [18] Cf. 1 *Ioan.*, 2:1.   [19] Cf. 1 *Tim.*, 3:15.
[20] Cf. Bonif. IX, *Ab origine mundi*, d. d. VII Oct. a. MCCCXCI; Callist. III, *Summus Pontifex*, d. d. I Ian. a. MCCCCLVI; Pius II, *Triumphans Pastor*, d. d. XXII Apr. MCCCCLIX; Innoc. XI, *Triumphans Pastor*, d. d. III Oct. a. MDCLXXVIII.

[21] *Ephes.*, 2:19-22.   [22] *Matth.*, 18:20.   [23] *Act.*, 2:42.
[24] *Coloss.*, 3:16.   [25] S. Augustin., *Epist.* 130, *ad Probam*, 18.
[26] *Missale Rom.*, Praef. Nativ.
[27] I. Card. Bona, *De divina psalmodia*, cap. 19, § III, 1.
[28] *Missale Rom.*, Secreta feriae V post Dom. II Quadrag.
[29] Cf. *Marc.*, 7:6 et *Is.*, 29:13.   [30] 1 *Cor.*, 11:28.
[31] *Missale Rom.*, Feria IV Cinerum: orat. post imposit., cinerum.
[32] *De praedestinatione sanctorum*, 31.
[33] Cf. S. Thom., *Summa Theol.*, II-II, q. LXXXII, a. 1.
[34] Cf. 1 *Cor.*, 3:23.   [35] *Hebr.*, 10:19-24.   [36] Cf. 2 *Cor.*, 6:1.
[37] Cf. *C. I. C.*, can. 125, 126, 565, 571, 595, 1367.
[38] *Coloss.*, 3:11.   [39] Cf. *Gal.*, 4:19.
[40] *Ioan.*, 20:21.   [41] *Luc.*, 10:16.   [42] *Marc.* 16:15-16.
[43] *Pontif. Rom.*, De ordinatione presbyteri, in manuum unctione.
[44] *Enchiridion*, cap. 3.   [45] *De gratia Dei* "Indiculus".
[46] S. Augustin., *Epist.* 130, *ad Probam*, 18.
[47] Cf. Const. *Divini cultus*, d. d. XX Dec. a. MCMXXVIII.
[48] Const. *Immensa*, d. d. XXII Ian. MDLXXXVIII.
[49] *C. I. C.*, can. 253.   [50] Cf. *C. I. C.*, can. 1257.
[51] Cf. *C. I. C.*, can. 1261.   [52] Cf. *Matth.*, 28:20.
[53] Cf. Pius VI, Const. *Auctorem fidei*, d. d. XXVIII Aug. MDCCXCIV, nn. XXXI-XXXIV, XXXIX, LXII, LXVI, LXIX-LXXIV.
[54] Cf. *Ioan.*, 21:15-17.   [55] *Act.*, 20:28.   [56] *Psalm*, 109, 4.
[57] *Ioan.*, 13:1.   [58] Conc. Trid., Sess. XXII, c. 1.   [59] *Ibidem*, c. 2.
[60] Cf. S. Thom., *Summa Theol.*, III. q. XXII, a. 4.
[61] Ioan. Chrys., *In Ioan. Hom.*, 86, 4.   [62] *Rom.*, 6:9.
[63] Cf. *Missale Rom.*, Praefatio.   [64] Cf. *Ibidem*, Canon.
[65] *Marc.*, 14:23.   [66] *Missale Rom.*, Praefatio.
[67] 1 *Ioan.*, 2:2.   [68] *Missale Rom.*, Canon.
[69] S. Augustin., *De Trinit.*, lib. XIII, c. 19.
[70] *Hebr.*, 5:7.   [71] Cf. Sess. XXII, c. 1.   [72] Cf. *Hebr.*, 10:14.
[73] S. Augustin., *Enarr. in Ps. CXLVII*, n. 16. [74] *Gal.*, 2:19, 20.
[75] Litt. Encycl. *Mystici Corporis*, d. d. XXIX Iun. MCMXLIII.
[76] *Missale Rom.*, Secreta Dom. IX post Pentec.
[77] Cf. Sess. XXII, c. 2 et can. 4.   [78] Cf. *Gal.*, 6:14.
[79] *Mal.*, 1:11.   [80] *Philipp.*, 2:5.   [81] *Gal.*, 2:19.
[82] Cf. Conc. Trid., Sess. XXIII, c. 4.
[83] Cf. Robertus Bellarm., *De Missa*, II, cap. 4.
[84] *De Sacro Altaris Mysterio*, III, 6.
[85] *De Missa*, I, cap. 27.   [86] *Missale Rom.*, Ordo Missae.
[87] *Ibidem*, Canon Missae.   [88] *Missale Rom.*, Canon Missae.
[89] 1 *Petr.*, 2:5.   [90] *Rom.*, 12:1.   [91] *Missale Rom.*, Canon Missae.
[92] *Pontif. Rom.*, De Ordinatione presbyteri.
[93] *Ibidem*, De altaris consecrat., Praefatio.
[94] Cf. Conc. Trid., Sess. XXII, c. 5.   [95] *Gal.*, 2:19-20.
[96] Cf. *Serm.*, CCLXXII.   [97] Cf. 1 *Cor.*, 12:27.   [98] Cf. *Eph.*, 5:30.
[99] Cf. S. Robertus Bellarm., *De Missa*, II, cap. 8.
[100] Cf. *De Civ. Dei*, lib. X, cap. 6.
[101] *Missale Rom.*, Canon Missae.   [102] Cf. 1 *Tim.*, 2:5.
[103] Litt. Encycl. *Certiores effecti*, d.d. XIII Nov. a. MDCCXLII, § 1.
[104] Conc. Trid., Sess. XXII, can. 8.   [105] 1 *Cor.*, 11:24.
[106] *Missale Rom.*, Collecta Festi Corp. Christi.   [107] Sess. **XXII, c. 6.**

[108] Litt. Encycl. *Certiores effecti*, § 3.   [109] Cf. Luc., 14:23.
[110] 1 *Cor.*, 10:17.   [111] Cf. S. Ignat. Martyr., *Ad Ephes.*, 20.
[112] *Missale Rom.*, Canon Missae.   [113] *Ephes.*, 5:20.
[114] *Missale Rom.*, Postcommunio Dominicae infra Oct. Ascens.
[115] *Ibidem*, Postcommunio Dominicae I post Pentec.
[116] *C. I. C.*, can. 810.   [117] Lib. IV, cap. 12.
[118] Dan., 3:57.   [119] Cf. Ioan., 16:23.
[120] *Missale Rom.*, Secreta Missae SS. Trinit.   [121] Ioan., 15:4.
[122] Conc. Trid., Sess. XIII, can. 1.
[123] Conc. Constant. II, *Anath. de trib. Capit.*, can. 9 collat. Conc. Ephes., *Anath. Cyrill.*, can. 8. Cf. Conc. Trid., Sess. XIII, can. 6; Pius VI, Const. *Auctorem fidei*, n. LXI.
[124] Cf. *Enarr. in Ps. XCVIII*, 9.   [125] *Apoc.*, 5:12 coll. VII, 10.
[126] Cf. Conc. Trid., Sess. XIII, c. 5 et can. 6.
[127] *In I ad Cor.*, 24:4.   [128] Cf. 1 *Petr.*, 1:19.   [129] *Matth.*, 11:28.
[130] Cf. *Missale Rom.*, Coll. in Missa Ded. Eccl.
[131] *Missale Rom.*, Seq. *Lauda Sion* in festo Ssmi. Corporis Christi.
[132] Luc., 18:1.   [133] *Hebr.*, 13:15.   [134] Cf. *Act.*, 2, 1-15.
[135] *Ibidem*, 10:9.   [136] *Ibidem*, 3:1.   [137] *Ibidem*, 16:25.
[138] *Rom.*, 8:26.   [139] S. Augustin., *Enarr. in Ps. LXXXV*, n. 1.
[140] S. Benedict., *Regula Monachorum*, c. XIX.   [141] *Hebr.*, 7:25.
[142] *Explicatio in Psalterium*. Praefatio; ut legitur in ed. P. L., LXX, 10. Nonnulli tamen censent partem huius dictionis non esse Cassiodoro tribuendam.   [143] S. Ambros., *Enarrat. in Ps. I*, n. 9.
[144] *Exod.*, XXXI, 15.   [145] *Confess.*, lib. IX, cap. 6.
[146] S. Augustin., *De Civ. Dei*, lib. VIII, cap. 17. [147] *Coloss.*, 3:1-2.
[148] S. Augustin., *Enarr. in Ps. CXXIII*, n. 2.   [149] *Hebr.*, 13:8.
[150] S. Thom., *Summa Theol.*, III, q. XLIX et q. LXII, art. 5.
[151] Cf. *Acta*, 10:38.   [152] *Eph.*, 4:13.
[153] *Missale Rom.*, Collecta III Missae pro plur. Martyr extra T. P.
[154] S. Beda Vener., *Hom. subd. LXX in solemn. omnium Sanct.*
[155] *Missale Rom.*, Collecta S. Ioan. Damascen.
[156] S. Bern., *Sermo II in festo omnium Sanct.*   [157] Luc., 1:28.
[158] "Salve Regina".   [159] S. Bern., *In Nativ. B.M.V.*, 7.
[160] *Hebr.*, 10:22.   [161] *Ibidem*, 10:21.   [162] *Ibidem*, 6:19.
[163] *C. I. C.*, can. 125.   [164] Cf. Ioan., 14:2.   [165] Ioan., 3:8.
[166] Cf. Iac., 1:17.   [167] *Ephes.* 1:4.
[168] Cf. Litt. Apost. Motu Proprio *Tra le sollecitudini*, d. d. XXII Novem. a. MCMIII.   [169] *Psalm.* 68:10; Ioan., 2:17.
[170] Suprema S. Congr. S. Officii: Decretum d. d. XXVI Maii MCMXXXVII.
[171] Cf. Pius X, Litt. Apost. Motu Proprio *Tra le sollecitudini*.
[172] Cf. Pius X, *loc. cit.*; Pius XI, Const. *Divini cultus*, II, V.
[173] Pius XI, Const. *Divini cultus*, IX.
[174] S. Augustin., *Serm. CCCXXXVI*, n. 1.
[175] *Missale Rom.*, Praefatio.
[176] Cf. S. Ambros., *Hexameron*, III, 5, 23.
[177] Cf. *Act.*, 4:32.   [178] *C. I. C.*, can. 1178.
[179] Pius XI, Const. *Divini cultus*.
[180] Cf. S. Augustin., *Tract. XXVI in Ioan.*, 13.
[181] Cf. Matth., 13:24-25.   [182] Litt. Encycl. *Mystici Corporis*.
[183] Ioel 2:15-16.   [184] 1 *Thess.*, 5:19.   [185] *Ibidem*, 5:21.
[186] *Hebr.*, 13:17.   [187] 1 *Cor.*, 14:33.   [188] *Apoc.*, 5:13.